BOYS

ON THE MARGIN

PROMOTING BOYS' LITERACY LEARNING AT KEY STAGE 2

Published by

Centre for Literacy in Primary Education

Webber Street

London SE1 8QW

Telephone: 020 7401 3382/3

Fax: 020 7928 4624

email:info@clpe.co.uk

website:www.clpe.co.uk

ISBN 1872267 40 8

Printed and bound in the UK

Photography: Phil Polglaze and Olivia O'Sullivan

Printed by: Print Data

Design: Chris Hyde

September 2004

BOYS
ON THE MARGIN

PROMOTING BOYS' LITERACY LEARNING AT KEY STAGE 2

KIMBERLY SAFFORD

OLIVIA O'SULLIVAN

AND

MYRA BARRS

FOREWORD

CLPE's publication *Boys and Writing* highlighted a number of common factors in successful initiatives for supporting boys' literacy learning.

These included:

- an emphasis on social approaches to literacy (and the role of formal and informal networks in supporting literacy learners);
- a greater role for ICT in promoting literacy learning;
- the encouragement of more reflective and personal approaches to reading and writing, with a strong emphasis on the role of talk in literacy learning;
- a recognition of the importance of graphic forms of planning for writing (eg drawing and mapping).

The *Promoting Boys' Literacy Learning at Key Stage 2* classroom research project, principally funded by the Esmée Fairbairn Foundation, enabled CLPE to promote some of these approaches systematically in a number of Key Stage 2 classes where teachers were prepared to try out these ways of working and observe the outcomes.

Some of most thought-provoking work in the field of gender and literacy has been done through teachers' action research, or through small-scale research in which researchers have worked closely with teachers. In these contexts the researchers have been able to look in depth at the literacy climate of a classroom and the difference it can make to the achievement of boys (and girls) in the class. Gemma Moss's *Fact and Fiction Project* (1999), the work of Eve Bearne (2002), Elaine Millard (1997), Hilary Minns (1991), and that of Lynda Graham with Croydon teachers (1999, 2003), have significantly enhanced our sense of the possible in this field.

The *Promoting Boys' Literacy Learning at Key Stage 2* project set out to make a difference to boys' achievement. Teachers involved in the project were invited to attend INSET and gain additional knowledge and skills through their participation. They were supported in the classroom by the project officer, who also observed the effects of the approaches they were using on boys' literacy learning. This was interventive research which aimed to see if the successful approaches that had been identified in other contexts could work in the project classrooms. Like CLPE's work in *The Reader in the Writer* (2001), the project highlighted the role of texts in literacy learning, and the place of drama in bringing

texts alive. A major feature of this new project was the 'drama on paper' that went on, in the shape of email conversations in role between pupils in the participating classes and the project officer.

Throughout the research the project focused on 'can but don't' boys; the group of boys who are at risk in school and who may make little progress because they are simply not getting enough practice in literacy. While they may not have major literacy difficulties, these 'boys on the margin' can get overlooked in school. Compared with their peers, they do not engage readily with literacy activities. They may be avoiding literacy work so as to disguise their difficulties or lack of confidence in literacy. They are turned off.

The project set out to engage these pupils in literacy learning, in the knowledge that learning is underpinned by the learner's involvement in, and attitudes to learning, and to oneself as a learner. Recent research by the NFER found that children's enthusiasm for reading had declined in recent years. Dr Marian Sainsbury (2003) of the NFER observed that it was possible that this was related to the national drive to improve standards: "Children are learning skills, reading material that has usually been chosen by the teacher rather than the children themselves. There may have been less emphasis on the sheer pleasure to be gained from books. Current guidance to teachers places great stress on fostering this enthusiasm and enjoyment". The decline of enthusiasm for reading in this country seems to be quite general. The 2001 *Progress in International Reading Literacy Study* (PIRLS) (Mullis et al 2003)), while finding that primary pupils in England were better at reading than those in almost any other country, also found that they were less confident about their ability and did not enjoy reading. English children came third in the study of reading achievement but ranked 34th out of 35 in relation to the enjoyment of reading.

The CLPE project did not settle for a reductionist definition of literacy. In order to become engaged with reading and writing pupils need a curriculum which goes beyond functional literacy. Reading and writing progress depend on more thoughtful, reflective and critical involvement with texts. The creative and interpretative nature of reading is recognised in a recent Demos paper on *Creative Reading* (Holden 2004), which also points to the way in which reading can be a transforming personal experience.

FOREWORD

We take what a writer gives us and we make it our own. We do not only gain knowledge from reading, we acquire emotional depth and subtlety of response. We can become more empathetic...the therapeutic value of reading in hospitals is well established.

Jon Scieszka, the author of a string of hugely popular books for children, says it a little differently on his website, in relation to his campaign GUYS READ:

A lot of what readers do in reading fiction is to imagine what other people think and feel. Studies of the psychology of boys have identified this as exactly what we need to help boys do – imagine what others think and feel, and then work on describing how you think and feel. Boys can obviously become better students if they can better use the tool of reading. But more importantly, they can become better people by expanding their emotional world and ability to empathize.

The education of the emotions goes hand in hand with literacy education. In order to become more thoughtful readers and writers we must also learn to empathise and to imagine.

This kind of view challenges a consensus which has developed in recent years in discussions of boys and literacy, a consensus which has been described as: "keep it short, keep it sharp, keep it finite" (Daly 2002). This idea that boys take to literacy learning more readily if it is presented to them in 'bite-size chunks' did not correspond to our findings in this project. Nor did the idea that boys prefer non-fiction texts seem to fit the facts. On the contrary, it was only when teachers allowed more time to explore really involving texts, and time to develop writing, that the boys we were observing began to make visible progress.

The project helped to give participating teachers the confidence to allow children more time to learn in literacy lessons. They were surprised at the outcomes. "In the case of *What Has Happened to Lulu?*, I was astonished that so much work could come from one poem" said a project teacher, speaking one year on from the end of the project. The same teacher described the way in which the behaviour of some of his case study boys had improved dramatically, apparently as a direct consequence of their participation in the project.

"The fact that I was focusing on a particular group of boys led me to give them roles in the class that I hadn't done before. It made me realise that I should have stretched them more previously....J. could at times be fairly irritating – cool, full of show, with other children looking up to him, yet never working to his potential. He's now the class representative on the school council....Last week he showed our MP round the school. He was confident, eloquent and informative. He's got the success bug and has a lot to be proud of."

Most of the project teachers have continued to work in similar ways since the project ended, and have introduced these approaches to their colleagues. They have found that, while the project helped them to focus on the achievement of boys, the implementation of it benefited all the children in the class and led to more enthusiasm for work in literacy.

Although the case study boys did make substantial progress on the CLPE Writing Scales in the course of the project, their results on Qualifications and Curriculum Authority (QCA) writing tests did not necessarily reflect either this progress or their teachers' judgements about how they had developed as writers. In order to help teachers to track the gradual positive moves that these children were making, the project team developed two checklists, one of the *Characteristics of Improving Writers,* and one of the *Characteristics of Improving Texts.*

The gap between teachers' assessments and performance on official tests reflected the difference between writing which is done for high stakes assessment, with little or no preparation, and writing in which the mind and feelings are engaged and which is the result of experience, discussion, and preparation. A major lesson from this classroom-based research is the value of adequate preparation for writing, particularly through talk, but also through drama and through graphic means of mapping stories, such as 'mindmaps' or storyboards. Assessment which judges children's progress by their performance in one-off, unprepared short writing tasks has no such chance of discovering what they can do.

Myra Barrs, CLPE

ACKNOWLEDGMENTS

We thank the teachers whose work, commitment and feedback animated this project

Paul Armstrong
Katie Brown
Gill Dove
Judith Herbert
Leonie Jones
Suzy Midgley

We also thank headteachers, support staff and children of the project schools

Brunswick Park, *Southwark*
Michael Faraday, *Southwark*
Sir James Barrie, *Wandsworth*
Wormholt Park, *Hammersmith and Fulham*

The poem 'What Has Happened to Lulu?' is taken from
Collected Poems for Children by Charles Causley (Macmillan 1996).
It is here reproduced by permission of David Higham Associates.

We are grateful for the support and guidance of our steering committee

Gemma Moss of the London Institute of Education
Margaret Meek Spencer of the London Institute of Education
Sue Pidgeon of the National Primary Strategy

The *Promoting Boys' Literacy Learning at Key Stage 2* project
was generously funded by
The Esmée Fairbairn Foundation
The Mercers' Company and The Reuters Foundation

CONTENTS

1
INTRODUCTION

Boys on the Margin: Promoting Boys' Literacy Learning at Key Stage 2 is the result of a research project in four inner London primary schools carried out by the Centre for Literacy in Primary Education. The project was prompted by the persistent underachievement of boys in primary school literacy (Ofsted 1993, Ofsted 1996, DfES 2003a) and the need to address this in ways that are practical for, and supportive of, class teachers. The research aim was to find out whether a number of specific teaching approaches could improve the motivation and performance of boys who are underachieving in literacy. These teaching approaches all involved oral and interactive approaches to literacy, and included using drama and communicating through ICT.

This project followed from earlier CLPE investigations into gender differences in reading, writing and achievement in literacy. CLPE's publications in this field have included a book of essays on the subject, *Reading the Difference* (Barrs & Pidgeon 1993), and two books based on action research studies by teachers: *Boys & Reading* (Barrs & Pidgeon 1998) and *Boys & Writing* (Barrs & Pidgeon 2002). Building on this previous work, *Boys on the Margin* examines the place of oracy and interaction in literacy development, and enquires into whether active and enactive approaches to learning literacy can successfully engage underachievers. As with previous studies, the aim of this enquiry is both to increase understanding of gender differences in literacy and to translate that understanding into effective pedagogy.

Growing concerns, national responses

Since the 1990s, the analysis of Key Stage literacy test results has precipitated what can only be described as a growing panic over boys' underachievement. In national Key Stage Two tests for English in 2003, the percentage of boys achieving the expected attainment levels for writing (Level 4) was unchanged from 2002 at 52%, while attainment levels in reading increased only marginally, from 77% to 78%. The results were a continuation of earlier trends. Although of course statistics for LEAs and individual schools vary from the national picture, girls have consistently achieved higher results in these tests.

From the DfES: National Key Stage Two Tests in English

	Boys		Girls		
	2002	2003	2002	2003	Gap *
Key Stage 1 (age 7)					
English					
Reading	81	80	88	88	8
Writing	82	76	90	87	11
Key Stage 2 (age 11)					
English	70	70	79	80	10
Reading	77	78	83	84	6
Writing	52	52	68	69	17
Maths	73	73	73	72	-1
Science	86	86	87	87	1

* The percentage points superiority of girls over boys

One project headteacher reported to CLPE that *"our results are so poor because of our boys – if it weren't for them we would be doing all right."* In a high stakes testing culture, teachers may feel understandably demoralised at pupils' apparent lack of progress. Boys are now routinely targeted as the problem needing remediation, both nationally and locally.

At the national level, the response to boys' underachievement has been twofold, and sometimes contradictory: the promotion of "boy friendly pedagogy" has been combined with a crackdown on "negative aspects of a school's culture that might have been created by boys" (DfES 2003b page 4). The DfES Toolkit in Using the National Healthy School Standard to Raise Boys' Achievement (DfES 2003b: 37) offers "25 hints and tips" to help raise boys' achievement. Only 7 of these 25 hints and tips have to do with teaching approaches, the rest all have to do with confronting "the negative aspects of boy culture" such as "bullying, name-calling and sexual harassment", "anti-swot culture" and "peer pressure" and with managing boys' behaviour. The list includes: "Give regular positive feedback and rewards", "Challenge stereotypes" and "Develop a whole school seating policy". Similarly, Ofsted (2003:22) says that a "non-macho ethos that values writing" is a major factor in boys' literacy achievement. The prevailing view of boys as learners here appears to be based on a deficit model, and very few *positive* aspects of boy culture seem to be noted.

The DfES Toolkit hints and tips which are curriculum-related promote ways of teaching which are

The DfES Tool Kit

This following checklist represents a simplified list of strategies taken from Gary Wilson's *Raising Boys' Achievement*.

- Develop policies that will address the negative aspects of boy culture including bullying, name calling and sexual harassment
- Involve pupils in policy development and review
- Begin lessons with a clear statement of learning outcomes
- Analyse resources for gender bias
- Investigate preferred learning styles
- Deliver work in time-limited, bite size chunks
- Provide challenge, competition and short term goals
- Give regular positive feedback and rewards
- Allow time for reflection and review
- Use peer support for learning
- Develop a whole school seating policy
- Regard an anti-swot culture as a major threat to equal opportunities
- Challenge stereotypes
- Consult pupils on a wide range of issues curricular, extra curricular and pastoral
- Establish a school council
- Provide academic mentoring in a range of ways and at various stages of school life
- Provide counselling on the same basis, including peer counselling
- Give pupils pastoral support roles
- Explore teachers' understanding of issues related to boys' underachievement
- Draw up a parents' skill register
- Map out individual pupil assessment statistics against precious data
- Negotiate targets with pupils individually
- Tie targets to strategies
- Deal explicitly with gender issues in PSHE including peer pressure and sexual harassment as well as developing personal skills such as cooperation and negotiation

Teaching and Learning

To what extent do patterns of curriculum, teaching and learning contribute to the disparity of achievement between boys and girls?

- Contributions from boys are prominent both physically and verbally during classroom interaction. Boys have more experience than girls of having their contributions evaluated during classroom interaction.
- However patterns of classroom interaction may have fewer implications for pupils' performance than the development of attitudes and strategies - in order to make a real difference to the issue it must be acknowledged that the most intervention takes place at a classroom level.
- Girls do better than boys on sustained tasks that are open-ended, process based, related to realistic situations, and that require pupils to think for themselves.
- Boys show greater adaptability to more traditional approaches to learning which require memorising abstract, unambiguous facts and rules that have to be acquired quickly. They appear willing to sacrifice deep understanding, requiring sustained effort, for solutions achieved at speed.

(source: DfES Gender and Achievement website: 'Understanding Gender and Achievement') www.standards.dfes.gov.uk/genderandachievement

thought to be more effective with boys. These include: "Deliver work in time-limited, bite-size chunks" and "Provide challenge, competition and short-term goals." The DfES Gender and Achievement website also makes reference to "literacy strategies targeted at boys' preferred learning styles." These are described as: "traditional approaches" and "memorising abstract, unambiguous facts and rules" because, according to the DfES, boys are "willing to sacrifice deep understanding" in order to learn at speed.

The National Literacy Strategy (1998) should theoretically support some of boys' "preferred learning styles", with its emphasis on a brisk pace, explicit teaching objectives, coverage of a wide range of genres (including information texts which boys are thought to favour over narrative texts) and specific short- and long-term targets. Indeed according to Noble and Bradford (2000) the Literacy Strategy should help boys "disproportionately" compared to girls. However, despite five years of the National Literacy Strategy, boys' literacy scores persistently lag behind those of girls, especially in writing.

The 2003 Key Stage Two writing tests included for the first time short, non-narrative writing tasks that may have been intended to cater for boys' preferred genres and to favour their interests. In Year 6, the test involved writing an advertisement about a new toy as imagined by the writer, and in Year 5 it featured instructional writing about space boots (QCA 2003). Yet the percentage of boys achieving Level 4 and above in the statutory assessments showed no gains over the 2002 results. Of course, girls did not make gains in this area either and, nationally, girls do not perform as well in writing as they do in reading. Yet (it is perhaps worth noting) girls' results do not appear to be generating policy publications or toolkits.

Hardening stereotypes

In researching and working with teachers and children, an underlying tendency of CLPE's work in gender and literacy has been to pose an alternative interpretation to what has often become an increasingly narrow view of how boys learn and what they are capable of learning. This kind of restricted view threatens to stunt the discussion of gender differences in literacy. Whereas historically there has been a positive drive for inclusion and equal opportunities for girls in education, underachieving boys, particularly ethnic minority boys, are increasingly segregated – on low-ability tables, in bottom set streams and on special educational needs registers (Baxter 2001, UK Audit Commission 2002, Alloway et al 1996:4, Galt 2000).

Hardening stereotypes of boys as reluctant, resistant or weak readers and writers have shaped a range of policy responses to underachievement that risk pathologising boys as virtually un-teachable – or teachable in only within narrow parameters, in "bite-sized chunks". In contrast, our project set out to involve boys in active and creative approaches to literacy, and to emphasise the value of extended work around texts. These approaches had proved successful in the previous action research studies coordinated by CLPE.

A changing policy landscape

At the beginning of our project, our aims were to inquire into and observe the interactive process of becoming literate through various forms of oral rehearsal for writing. CLPE's research was also designed to foreground neglected areas of the National Curriculum for English (Drama, and Speaking and Listening) and to create opportunities for teachers to act, in smaller or larger ways, outside of their perceived and real curriculum constraints. But in the course of the research year, the national climate began to change. The government started sending unequivocal signals to schools that they should not feel constrained in their teaching and planning. A series of central education policy and curriculum documents urged schools and teachers to become more creative and to make more use of oral and interactive approaches to teaching and learning (QCA 2003a, Ofsted 2003a, DfES 2003). The QCA (2003b) published extensive schemes of work, teaching aims and desirable outcomes for Speaking and Listening. The new Primary Strategy document

Excellence and Enjoyment (DfES 2003) stated unequivocally that the National Literacy Strategy was not statutory and that teachers "have the power to decide how they teach" (ibid.16:2.7).

Our CLPE project had reflected a growing awareness that more creative approaches to literacy might be required if persistent underachievement was to be tackled effectively. Recent policies favouring creativity, and the Primary Strategy directive that schools should "take control of their curriculum" (ibid.16:2.4), are to be welcomed. However, discussions with teachers since the appearance of *Excellence and Enjoyment* have suggested that many feel unsure how to carry out these new initiatives in the classroom.

Teachers may also legitimately feel unclear about how 'creativity' fits into the current model of statutory, summative assessment. Many schools now devote a substantial part of Year 6 to coaching children for the Key Stage 2 statutory tests, and have seen their SATs results rise as a direct consequence. Whilst these schools may want to spend less time in teaching to the test, they are still subject to pressure from test scores, targets and league tables. Creative pedagogies involving oracy can have a positive impact on boys' underachievement. However, these gains may not be immediately apparent in their performance in external tests, however obvious they are to their teachers. Questions about appropriate forms of assessment emerged strongly as our project proceeded. Other questions also guided our enquiry. How might teachers integrate oracy into current pedagogic paradigms? Is there an alternative view to that of boys as deficit learners? How does ICT engage boys, and in what circumstances? These intertwining strands of questioning form the basis of the chapter that follows, which contains a review of the research and policy themes in these areas.

2

GENDER AND UNDERACHIEVEMENT

THEMES FROM RESEARCH

In the space of fifteen years, gender equality issues in education have shifted considerably. Concerns about access and opportunities for girls have been superseded by concerns about the underperformance of boys. Girls are now generally perceived as the 'superior' partners in the educational equation (White 1996: 100, Baxter 2001) Some educational consultants (Hannan 2003) have even gone as far as to assert that "Boys need a higher quality of teaching and learning than girls" in order to redress this educational inequality.

Discussions of gender differences in literacy often take as their starting point the assumption that girls are advantaged in literacy because of their greater exposure to and familiarity with narrative texts and poetry. This assumption has even entered analysis of Key Stage literacy test results (Green & Green 2000). However a range of other research is persuasively challenging this view by examining patterns of avoidance and resistance among boys, and highlighting boys' concerns about peer group status (Moss 1999, 1999a). Other studies have looked at boys' and girls' literacy outside school through investigations of family literacies (Rundell 2001), and compared children's perceived relevance of school literacy to a range of literacy practices outside school (Street 2003, Smith & Wilhelm 2002). Teachers' expectations and strong stereotyping of boys and of girls can be at odds with children's own self-images as readers and writers (Holden 1999, Myhill 1999).

Recent research in early years settings has pointed to the way in which boys' narrative fantasy development is often quashed for appearing 'inappropriate' (Holland 2003: 31). This research theorises that blocking access to 'taboo play themes' may cause boys to lose interest in subsequent school literacy. Boys seem to be less experienced in the socialising around literacy that appears to help many girls become confident readers and writers (Barrs 2000, Moss 1999). However, boys may be discouraged from networking around their preferred texts in school if their interests are considered inappropriate or even deviant. Michael Anderson (2003), one of few primary teachers to engage publicly with the violent media that seems to fascinate many boys, has documented his attempts to enlist these in their literacy learning.

Pedagogy or behaviour management?

In recent years education policy has tended to focus on what is to be taught as a universal entitlement for all children. This very heavy emphasis on instruction has downgraded questions of how children can *learn* what is to be taught. In such a context, where all the emphasis is on 'delivering' the curriculum, behaviour management may become a substitute for pedagogy.

The behaviour management of boys is a dominant theme in policies to tackle their underachievement (Ofsted 1993, 2003, DfES 2003b). This focus on behaviour supports perceptions that boys will actively resist the offered curriculum and must be controlled in order to learn it. A DfES/Cambridge project (Younger & Warrington 2003) highlights behaviour agreements, positive discipline, parent/community links and strong mentoring as factors in steering boys to success within the national strategies and assessment frameworks. Fischer (2002) likewise includes "a clear sense of order and discipline" as an effective teaching strategy to improve boys' writing. While these issues are not unrelated to raising boys' achievement in school, we would suggest that an emphasis on controlling behaviour may sideline potentially effective pedagogies, some of which have been promoted in our project. These include opportunities for children to talk, to interact, and to learn through doing, making and discussing. In a climate where all the focus is on control, opportunities like these may be curtailed.

In interviews with Wood (2001: 11) primary teachers evaluated pupils' gender differences in relation to a number of curriculum imperatives: the need for classroom order; the need to progress through curriculum content that is highly prescriptive in terms of pacing, sequencing and content; the need to prepare children for the next stage and to demonstrate progress and achievement in relation to a range of targets and performance indicators. Girls were perceived as adapting more easily to what is required. While teachers in Wood (ibid:9) said that they expected boys and girls to achieve the same results, they simultaneously identified boys' preferences for visual, kinetic, active and hands-on learning as militating against this.

Despite the current heavy emphasis on targets as a means of boosting achievement, the increasing tendency of schools to teach directly to the tests may not always benefit boys. Citing evidence that primary schools since 1998 have used test results to dictate curriculum planning, Lamprianou and Boyle (2003) found that a significant number of schools actually had worse literacy test scores after spending more time teaching English during 2001-2002.

Intersections of race, gender, achievement and the curriculum

Although the underachievement of ethnic minority boys is well documented (Gillborn & Gipps 1996, Gillborn & Mirza 2000), there is relatively little research in primary settings into pupils' own views of how ethnicity and ethnic identity intersect with gender and underachievement (Connolly 1998, Epstein et al 2001, Reay 1991). Sewell's (1997) and Mac an Ghaill's (1994) portraits of boys in secondary school settings can be read as the outcomes of primary school experiences, yet readers of these studies can only guess at what went on in the years before Year 7. Tony Sewell's (op.cit.) researches have highlighted the way in which teachers may become insecure when black boys' behaviour appears too lively. He has pointed out how even basic physical movements - "boys' bodies in space" - can cause considerable anxiety for teachers.

Research in Birmingham (Warren & Gilborn 2003) concludes that the "colour blind" National Curriculum and National Literacy Strategy themselves are responsible for undermining high-quality anti-racism initiatives developed by the local authority that might otherwise positively impact on ethnic minority attainment. Issues of curriculum content are sharply foregrounded by this research.

Echoing themes in the DfES/Cambridge project (Younger & Warrington 2003), research in successful Lambeth schools (McKenley, Power, Ishani and Demi 2003) attributes the high attainment of Caribbean Heritage pupils in these schools to the school ethos, the regular celebration of pupils' identities, and to the presence of role models and learning mentors. However, the Lambeth research also tantalisingly alludes to a "mesmerising" curriculum – an "inclusive" and "multicultural" curriculum. Speaking at the conference *Raising Achievement of Black Caribbean Pupils*, on 14 November 2003, the report's co-author Louise Ishani reported that the "monitoring of pupils' learning styles to design tailored interventions" was a factor in raising Caribbean Heritage pupils' attainment. If policies are to affect the persistent underachievement of certain groups of pupils, curriculum content itself will have to be addressed, and the 'one-size-fits-all' approach of recent years may have to be modified.

The writing problem

Daly's (2002) comprehensive review of the range of research into strategies to improve boys' writing offers a unique map of a growing territory. As concerns about boys' attainment in writing have grown, strategies to address this issue have proliferated. Indeed, Daley's (ibid.) review for Ofsted (2003) can appear contradictory; for example, writing frames are described at different points as both effective and ineffective strategies.

For some time, national key stage tests have shown writing to be the biggest area of weakness in literacy for both boys and girls (Ofsted 2003, DfES 2003a). Writing is, of course, the most scrutinised 'product' of literacy education, subject to a detailed assessment checklist that includes handwriting, grammar, content and cohesion (QCA 2000, QCA 2003), all of which children must control under timed conditions. There is however a growing debate about the writing curriculum itself and whether this, and the related assessment tasks, are at the real root of boys' (and girls') underachievement.

In Grainger, Goouch & Lambirth (2003), children themselves describe their progressive alienation from writing as they experience decreasing choice and control over what and how they write in Key Stage Two. If "writers negotiate their place within the many communities of which they are a part, with a variety of resources and competing demands" (Applebee 2000), then it seems that boys, in particular, may have limited opportunities to bring their resources and interests into play as part of their writing at school.

Past approaches to teaching writing advocated that pupils' interests and ideas should be the starting point for writing. Graves (1983) argued for longer, more flexible preparation time for writing, and emphasised the importance of young writers choosing their own topics for writing. Smith (1982: 121-126) criticised the lack of time in schools for the "pre-writing" phase: "day-dreaming, searching, planning, making notes." Writing workshop approaches also emphasised the importance of topic choice, of writers pursuing their own interests, and of the creation of audiences for writing through reading aloud and publication. But in recent years concerns about meeting writing attainment targets have helped to create an increasingly sedentary writing curriculum, focused on the rapid learning and perform-ing of a number of written language genres.

ICT in and out of school

Boys are generally thought to respond positively to using ICT for learning (Noble & Bradford 2000). Because of this, McGuinn (2000) has asked whether ICT could "introduce those four magic words into boys' writing: 'context, purpose, audience and variety' ". Some educational researchers (Wood 2000) have called computers and writing "a marriage waiting to happen" – although he focuses almost exclusively on the drafting and transcription uses of the computer.

In the literacy curriculum, ICT is usually seen as a writing tool, and its potential uses for reading and discussion remain relatively unexplored in schools. However Neil Mercer and his colleagues (Dawes, Mercer & Wegerif 2000) created interactive software purposely for the discussion of PSHE and Citizenship themes as part of the *Thinking Together* project. These materials lend themselves to use in other contexts. In this CLPE project they were used to inform the development of software which would promote discussion around texts.

There appears to be a growing gap between ICT as children experience, learn and play with it outside of school and the use of ICT in school tasks (McFarlane et al 2002, Somekh & Mavers 2003). There have been only a few studies that have linked children's 'real' experiences of ICT to reading and writing in school. They include some small-scale studies of email as a literacy activity (Babbage 1999, Merchant 2003). Evidence from our project strongly suggests that, for many children, and boys in particular, ICT outside school is exploratory, fun, a chosen activity, and one that

involves much reading for pleasure. Our evidence also suggests that when ICT is integrated into the study of literature and the teaching of writing, children are likely to become much more effectively engaged with school literacy.

Knowledge about oracy

Good oral skills must be in place before children can develop well in reading and writing (Arnold 1997), and Barrs (2000) has called talk "the crucial halfway house between reading and writing". Talk may be used to learn more about a text, to inhabit and explore characters and dilemmas, to explicitly identify the way forward in planning and revising a piece of writ-ing, and to collaborate in writing. Goodwin (1999) in *The Articulate Classroom*, describes a range of talk for learning, drawing on the evidence that where two or more people pool their mental resources through the medium of talk, they can achieve more together than they ever could separately. Much of Aidan Chambers' work (1993) has illustrated how genuine teacher-pupil interaction around texts can be achieved. His examples show how questioning and discussion about a shared reading experience can gradually be led from more concrete to more abstract topics.

When the QCA (2003c) elicited a series of responses to the question of what speaking and listening ought to look like in schools, Cameron (2003: 64) argued that the current official interpretation of talk is overly narrow and utilitarian, and suggested the fore-grounding of a range of written and speech genres through talk, role play, drama and performance. Kempe (1999) also underlines the importance of enactment, arguing that: "Literacy involves a lot more than simply ascribing sound to marks on a page…. Enacting words reinforces their relationship with context and underlines the fact that marks on a page are incomplete notations of how humans communicate verbally". Heathcote (1980) described the value of drama in literacy development as the way in which it provides a "context and purpose for talk", demanding shifts of style, delivery, purpose of language and selection of vocabulary. Similarly Steele and Collins (in Barrs & Cork 2001: 222) discuss the value of drama in exploring a text – the way it enables children to use their own understanding and experience of the real world in conjunction with the imagined reality of the text.

However both talk and movement may be discouraged in some classrooms because of concerns about poor behaviour. Boys' talk and boys' movement may be particularly strongly discouraged, for some of the reasons identified by Tony Sewell and others. In contexts where opportunities for talk, enactment and drama are limited, the links between oracy and literacy may not be so easy to develop.

The forces against talk and movement in classrooms are powerful. Martin (1987: 20) makes explicit the fears that teachers may have about oracy's link to poor behaviour:

Is the class too noisy? Are the groups discussing anything worthwhile? What is worthwhile talk? What about the silent ones? Will people think my discipline is poor? Is a quiet class really a good learning situation? Is what the students want to talk about as important for them as what I want them to talk about? And so on. Once a teacher moves out of the traditional position of being the giver of questions and the receiver of right or wrong answers, there is no more certainty.

The *Promoting Boys' Literacy Learning at Key Stage 2* project found that because of these fears, children could often be routinely discouraged from talking and acting in class.

Many of the themes that have arisen in this chapter resonated in CLPE interviews with boys and teachers and in data from project classrooms. We drew on the work of some of the experts whose work is reviewed here in planning our interventions and in interpreting our data. The project began against a background in which its main themes were currently preoccupying many people in primary education, and in which strategies to address its key concerns were being developed. However it was also apparent that, in several classrooms, teachers felt that it was just too risky to deploy even those pedagogic approaches that they believed might make a difference to underachievers.

3

RESEARCH AND INTERVENTION

AN OVERVIEW OF THE BOYS' LITERACY LEARNING PROJECT

Over the two terms (January to July 2003) of the *Promoting Boys' Literacy Learning at Key Stage 2* project, six inner London teachers and their Year 4 and 5 classes engaged in a range of interactive approaches to literacy, through purposeful talk, oral rehearsal for writing, collaborative drafting and writing, peer support, forms of drama and using ICT for email, web publishing and interactive software to stimulate discussion. Three specific texts were used in order to compare pedagogical approaches, learning experiences and outcomes from the six classrooms. Teachers were supported by CLPE through INSET and regular in-class support and observation. A CLPE research officer recorded teaching and learning, literacy processes and outcomes, and drew together the different strands and experiences from the six classrooms for analysis and evaluation.

Project	School A	School B	School C	School D
	Year 5	Years 4 and 5	Years 4 and 5	Year 5
No. on role	430	326	515	462
SEN	168	87	100	200
Statements	4	7	15	15
EAL	304	173	267	200
FSM	161	174	273	275
Asylum Seekers			10	104

Project Schools' literacy in 2002 Key Stage 2 tests

School	Boys Reading	Girls Reading	Boys Writing	Girls Writing	Combined English Boys/Girls
School A	70%	86.6%	44%	56.6%	63% / 77%
School B	50%	83%	42%	77.7%	42.3% / 83.3%
School C	76%	68.75%	54%	41%	65% / 54.9%
School D	61.5%	77.4%	26.9%	51.6%	58% / 71%

% of children at Level 4 and above

The project's main funder was a charity with a strong record of support for programmes that promote inclusion and success in inner city schools. The criteria for participation in the project were that schools should be in areas of socio-economic deprivation and that Key Stage literacy test scores should be below the national average.

Accordingly, the intakes of the participating schools included high numbers of free school meals and children learning English as an additional language. One school had the highest number of asylum seekers in its education authority. Key Stage Two tests in English for three of the schools show a wide gap in attainment between girls and boys. In one school, boys outperformed girls and had been doing so over some time, but writing attainment overall was low and there was a large gap between reading and writing attainment for both boys and girls.

In the four Year 5 and two Year 4 classes, ethnic minority children were the overwhelming majority. Overall there were more ethnic minority boys than girls. Class size ranged from 22 to 29 pupils.

Class	Total	Girls	Boys	EM girls	EM boys	total EM
Teacher K Year 5	29	15	14	11	9	20/29
Teacher S Year 5	29	13	16	12	15	27/29
Teacher L Year 5	26	14	12	7	13	19/26
Teacher G Year 4	22	8	14	6	13	18/22
Teacher P Year 5	22	10	12	7	9	16/22
Teacher J Year 4	22	14	8	13	7	20/22

Three classes x 22
One class x 26
Two classes x 29

The Year 4 classes were particularly imbalanced: one class had 8 boys, 14 girls; one class had 8 girls, 14 boys (a ratio of 2:7)
Ethnic 'minority' children are the majority.
All classes had full time classroom assistants.

Although the Year 4 classes were particularly imbalanced (one had 8 girls and 14 boys, the other had 8 boys and 14 girls) the Year 5 classes were roughly equal in numbers of boys and girls. In some schools mobility was high, but the Year 4 and Year 5 boys chosen for case study had been in their schools from Reception or Year 1 and had good attendance over the two terms of the project.

Teachers ranged widely in experience, from those in their second and third years of teaching to those with 20 and 30 years of teaching experience. The six teachers included a deputy headteacher and a literacy coordinator. All had BA with QTS or PGCE qualifications, and

Teachers, gender & ethnicity	How long teaching	Responsibilities
G – white female	30 years	Literacy
P – white male	20 years	ICT, deputy head
L – white female	1 year	PSE
J – Caribbean Heritage female	12 years	PE
S – white female	8 years	Maths
K – white female	3 years	Gifted and Talented

two teachers had been on accredited courses at CLPE. Reasons for their participating in the project ranged from wanting to further their own understanding of the issues, to being involuntarily placed in the project by the headteacher for professional development.

Methodology and data collection

This project synthesised elements of formal research and teacher action research. Its goals were to add to overall understanding of gender differences in literacy, but also to devise practical knowledge and strategies that would be applicable to local situations and individuals. Teachers were asked to carry out specific pedagogic approaches which had been identified as being effective in other CLPE projects (Barrs & Cork 2001, Barrs & Pidgeon 1998 and 2002). These included using drama, peer support and collaboration to support the writing process, creating units of work around whole texts and working with story-telling to enrich oral language and narrative experiences.

The project researcher took an active role, working and liaising with teachers on a regular basis and observing teaching and learning. Methodology took as its starting point the naturalistic inquiry and purposeful sampling of Lincoln & Guba (1985), and Glaser & Strauss (1967), with the classroom as a prime example of how "realities are multiple, constructed and holistic, knower and known are interactive…all entities are in a state of mutual and simultaneous shaping." (Lincoln & Guba: op cit 37). As teachers carried out the interventions, a range of qualitative and quantitative data was collected over two terms.

The CLPE research officer visited each class weekly for two terms, to support teachers and to observe literacy teaching. The observations covered the timetabled one-hour Literacy session as a minimum, but would cover half a day where teachers organised extended sessions for writing or drama. The research team videotaped children and teachers in a range of literacy settings: drama, text enactment, reading, speaking and listening, and using ICT for discussion and for writing.

Boys and teachers were interviewed at the beginning of the project. The research officer carried out reflective interviews with a focus group of boys at the end of the project about their reading and their writing.

Reading records, reading journals and writing tasks – both from the interventions and from other class literacy work – were collected over two terms. Boys' writing included the QCA test papers for Years 4 and 5.

Teachers were invited to reflect on the research throughout the project, during INSET, in discussion or via email with the research officer. Teachers' planning was also collected, to observe how and when they integrated the project interventions into their literacy timetables.

The timeline of the project, which had to be carried out over two terms, was demanding on all participants, with teachers carrying out a range of interventions often in addition to their school and year group schemes of work:

The Spring term:

- INSET 1: introduction of the project , teaching approaches, texts and materials, introduction of CLPE software, drama training with Susanna Steele of Greenwich University.
- Collection of baseline data, teacher and pupil interviews, initial interventions for talk; classes develop talk activities; teachers introduce and develop a Charles Causley poem through discussion and drama

- INSET 2: introducing a traditional 'Selkie' story, in a retelling by Kevin Crossley-Holland.
- A range of writing carried out; project website is live
- Weekly observations, video recordings

The Summer term:

- INSET 3: introduce a contemporary novel by Louis Sachar. Feedback from teachers and writing analysis; teachers continue to develop oracy approaches to texts; weekly observations and video; web publishing
- QCA tests, teacher and pupil interviews, National Curriculum and CLPE assessments, writing conferences.

The project was guided by a steering committee of professionals and educators in the fields of literacy learning: Margaret Meek Spencer of the London Institute of Education, Gemma Moss of the London Institute of Education, Sue Pidgeon of the National Primary Strategy who met regularly to assess the project's progress and outcomes.

Research questions

Our initial research questions involved inquiring into the processes of oral rehearsal and interactivity in teaching and learning. We asked whether and how these approaches could make a positive difference to our case study boys' literacy learning and achievement:

- How does oral rehearsal - reading aloud, a range of discussion opportunities, and forms of drama - encourage underachieving boys to respond to texts and prepare for writing?

- How does creating a visible audience (through performance) or a virtual audience (using ICT) for reading and writing affect boys' perceptions of literacy and their achievement?

- How does collaboration and peer support help boys' literacy development?

The research team was interested in what would happen when teachers expanded the pre-writing phase of literacy teaching and learning. Would more time

spent in discussion and text enactment help underachievers, particularly boys, and would this expanded time enable teachers to find out more about underachievers' particular difficulties? What kinds of talk around texts would develop in classrooms? How would teachers manage talk for literacy and integrate ICT for discussion? When children got out of their chairs for drama, would this create disruption? As the project developed, secondary questions emerged:

- What is appropriate assessment for oral work (speaking and listening, and drama)?

- What is appropriate assessment for children in early, developmental stages of literacy?

Teachers and the research team would reflect on and try to answer these questions through two strands of intervention: texts and approaches.

Texts and approaches

Three texts were selected as a range of very different but powerful narratives that would lend themselves to discussion, reflective reading and creative responses:

- *What Has Happened to Lulu?* (a poem by Charles Causley)
- *The Seal Wife* (a traditional tale)
- *There's A Boy in the Girls' Bathroom* (a contemporary novel by Louis Sachar)

In this way, teachers would be able to work with progressively longer texts over two terms. Using three common texts allowed experiences and outcomes from classrooms to be usefully compared.

Through these texts, teachers would

- Develop oral rehearsal, including drama, in a range of settings

- Use ICT for interaction and communication with CLPE software linked to the intervention texts and publish children's work on the project website (for link see www.clpe.co.uk)

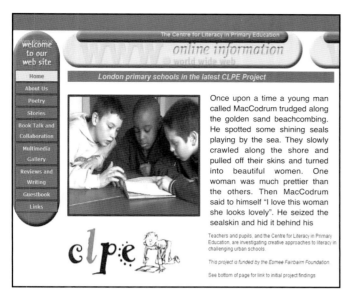

The Centre for Literacy in Primary Education
online information
world wide web

welcome to our web site

Home
About Us
Poetry
Stories
Book Talk and Collaboration
Multimedia Gallery
Reviews and Writing
Guestbook
Links

London primary schools in the latest CLPE Project

Once upon a time a young man called MacCodrum trudged along the golden sand beachcombing. He spotted some shining seals playing by the sea. They slowly crawled along the shore and pulled off their skins and turned into beautiful women. One woman was much prettier than the others. Then MacCodrum said to himself "I love this woman she looks lovely". He seized the sealskin and hid it behind his

Teachers and pupils, and the Centre for Literacy in Primary Education, are investigating creative approaches to literacy in challenging urban schools.

This project is funded by the Esmee Fairbairn Foundation.

See bottom of page for link to initial project findings

Through the three specific texts, teachers were asked to consider the ideas of Dawes, Mercer and Wegerif (2000) and Aidan Chambers (1993) and how these might be used in developing strategies for talk around texts in the classroom.

In the first INSET, teachers looked at the interactive software *Kate's Choice,* from the *Thinking Together* project (Dawes, Mercer & Wegerif op.cit.), which is used to stimulate discussion of the moral options and actions open to a girl who has caught her friend stealing. The CLPE research team was interested in extending this approach to discussions of texts. *Kate's Choice* became a loose model for interactive software which would enable children to discuss the dilemmas and choices that fictional characters in stories or poems might face, and to more fully imagine the characters and the world of the text. In conjunction with the software, Mercer's "rules for talk", which encourage children to reflect upon and justify their ideas in discussions, would be used in the more specific context of literacy, to support talk about texts, collaborative reading and writing.

Teachers were also introduced to Chambers 'Tell Me' questions (1993) about children's reading. Chambers conceptualises literacy learning as a dynamic process that builds on children's developing ideas and experiences. The questions he proposes for introducing discussion begin concretely with likes and dislikes, and move towards more abstract thinking and discussion about books, which involves the class in pinning down the central themes in a text. The research team was interested in the extent to which teachers would make

literacy a social activity by engaging in 'Book Talk', and whether boys would become more involved in school literacy through these discussions of reading.

Linked to 'Book Talk' was the observation by Gemma Moss (1999) that girls often network socially around books, reading and recommending texts to each other. Teachers were asked to consider how boys might be encouraged or directed to engage in the kind of informal, peer group socialising around literacy that appears to help many girls become confident readers and writers.

The research team was also interested in how teachers could develop drama as an effective oral approach to literacy. What kinds of drama were already taking place in classrooms and how were they linked to literacy? What did children think about drama, particularly boys?

All the intervention texts and approaches were well within the framework of the National Curriculum for English and the objectives of the National Literacy Strategy for the appropriate terms and year groups (DfEE 1998).

Teachers carried out interventions with the whole class; it was important for all participants in the project that boys were not withdrawn for special or separate teaching. The research team looked at commonalities and differences in teaching and learning across the six classrooms, tracked individual boys and drew together the different experiences, responses and results from the interventions in order to evaluate

- Boys' responses to different types of narrative texts
- Whether and how oral, interactive and collaborative approaches to literacy would support boys' interest in school literacy
- Any changes in boys' attitude and performance in literacy tasks as a result of the interventions

A focus group

Each teacher identified four boys in each class for observation. Originally all of the boys chosen were West African and Caribbean Heritage boys. These choices did reflect the schools' intakes to some extent, but teachers were asked to identify a wider range of boys for particular study.

The project's interventions were aimed at hard-to-reach boys, and these included:

- Boys who can read and write but choose not to
- Boys who read but choose not to write
- Boys with low literacy levels in comparison to their peers
- Boys who are active non-participants in school literacy

Of the 24 Year 4 and 5 boys identified by teachers, 12 were at National Curriculum Attainment Levels 2c-2a for reading and 18 were Level 2 or below for writing. Eighteen boys received free school meals and 21 were ethnic minorities.

The 24 boys were assessed at the beginning and at the end of the project, with National Curriculum attainment levels for reading and writing, and also with CLPE Reading and Writing Scales for ages 8-12 (page 26). These were compared with the levels on both of these measures for the whole class. The project researcher focused closely on a smaller group of Year 4 and Year 5 boys, to gain deeper insights into their apparent lack of interest or their underachievement in school literacy.

24 boys

White/ BSWNI*	Portuguese	Somali	West African	East African	Caribbean Heritage
3	2	4	5	1	9

Additional Literacy Support		School Action		School Action Plus	
2		7		1	

Languages

Somali	Portuguese	Twi	Yoruba	Creole	Arabic/French	Tigrinya
4	2	2	2	5	1	1

Stages of English

Stage 1	Stage 2	Stage 3	Stage 4
0	6	6	4

* Britain / Scotland / Wales / Northern Ireland

Focus boys	Year Group	Languages other than English (Stage of English)	Free School Meals	Learning Support
A	Year 4	Creole (5)	no	Additional Literacy Support (ALS) and School Action Plus
A	Year 4	Somali (2)	yes	School Action
O	Year 4	Creole (5)	no	ALS and School Action Plus
J	Year 5	None	yes	none
B	Year 5	Creole (3)	no	none
K	Year 5	Creole (5)	yes	School Action
Y	Year 5	Somali (3)	yes	School Action
C	Year 5	Portuguese (2)	no	none

Year 4	Jan NC Reading	Jan NC Writing	Jan CLPE Reading	Jan CLPE Writing	June NC Reading	June NC Writing	June CLPE Reading	June CLPE Writing
A	3c	2b	2	1	3a	2c	2	2
O	2c	1a	1	1	2b	2c	2	1/2
A	3c	2c	2	2	3b	2b	3	2
W	2a	2c	2	2	3b	2b	3	2
M	3c	2a	3	2	3b	3	3c	3
A	2b	2b	2	2	3b	3	2a	3
S	3b	3b	3	3	4	3	3a	3
D	3b	3b	3	3	4	3	3a	3

Year 5	Jan NC Reading	Jan NC Writing	Jan CLPE Reading	Jan CLPE Writing	June NC Reading	June NC Writing	June CLPE Reading	June CLPE Writing
J	2a	2b	2	2	Below L3	3b	3	4
K	2b	2b	2	2	3c	3b	3	2/3
O	2a	2b	2	2	3b	3b	3	2/3
Z	3b	2a	3	3	4c	3a	4	3
M	3c	3c	3	3	3a	4c	3	3
B	3a	2a	2	2	4c	3b	3	3
J	3a	3c	2	2	3a	3c	3	2/3
K	3c	3a	3	3	3b	4c	3/4	3/4
D	3c	3c	3	3	4b	3b	4	3/4
K	2a	2a	2	2	3b	3c	3	3
J	2a	2b	2	2	3c	3c	3	3
Y	2a	2c	2	2	3a	3b	3	2/3
A	2b	2a	2	1	2a	2a	2	2
V	3c	2b	3	2	3a	3c	3	3
A	3c	3c	2	3	2a	3c	3	3
C	3b	2b	3	3	3a	2a	3	3

Data from this project are overwhelmingly qualitative, and the numbers are small. However, it is the experiences of individual children and teachers that speak most eloquently, and urgently, about matters of teaching and learning. Throughout this report readers will hear the voices of individuals, boys and teachers, thinking aloud about reading and writing. Through boys' talk, enactment and writing, we may glimpse them in the process of becoming literate. As a group of teachers carry out common tasks and approaches, they also reflect on what is effective pedagogy. It is in these 'telling moments' that we believe this project illuminates wider possibilities for creative interaction in literacy teaching and learning that could raise the achievements of certain groups of children.

CLPE Writing Scale 1 Ages 6-8 years

Level	Description	NC level
Beginning writer 1	May be composing by dictating own texts, and may have some strategies for writing independently (eg drawing writing, copying, inventing own code), but still at an early stage of understanding how language is written down, and needing support with transcription.	1
Early writer 2	Gaining confidence in using writing for a range of personal purposes (eg messages, notices). Drawing on experiences of seeing language written down (eg in shared writing) and demonstrating more understanding of the alphabetic nature of the English writing system. Ready to have a go at writing independently, using a few early strategies for spelling (eg use of initial letters, some known words, using letter strings as 'place holders'), so that writing can be read back more consistently.	2c
Developing writer 3	Using a small range of writing (eg letters, lists, brief narratives) independently, but still needing help with extending and developing texts. May be drawing on models from reading in structuring own texts. Reading back own texts consistently, experimenting with punctuation, and developing strategies for spelling (eg known words, phonetically based invented spellings) which enable texts to be read by others.	2b
Moderately fluent writer 4	Writing more confidently and developing ideas at greater length in a few familiar forms. Growing ability to structure these texts; willing to experiment with a wider range of writing. Beginning to use punctuation to support meaning (eg full stops, exclamation marks). Drawing on a wider range of strategies in spelling (eg. common letters strings, awareness of visual patterns, as well as phonetically based spellings).	2a
Fluent writer 5	Growing independence in using writing for a wider range of purposes (eg expressive, informational, imaginative). Aware of different audiences and beginning to shape texts for a reader. Often chooses to write over longer periods. Punctuating texts for meaning more consistently. Writing shows increasing attention to the visual patterns in spelling.	3
Exceptionally fluent writer 6	A confident and independent writer who enjoys writing in different genres, and is developing a personal voice. Writing may show marked influences of texts that have been read. Drawing on a range of effective strategies for spelling and using standard forms more consistently. Using written language in more deliberate ways and making meanings more explicit. Still needs support in sustaining long pieces of writing or expressing complex meanings	4

©CLPE

CLPE Writing Scale 2 Ages 8-12 years

Level	Description	NC level
Inexperienced writer 1	Experience as a writer may be limited: may be composing orally with confidence but be reluctant to write or avoid taking risks with transcription. Needing a great deal of help with developing own texts (which are often brief) and with the writing demands of the classroom. Relying mainly on phonetic spelling strategies and memorised words, with few self-help strategies. Seldom using punctuation to mark meaning.	1-2c
Less experienced writer 2	Increasingly willing to take risks with both composition and transcription. Writing confidently in certain genres (eg simple narratives) and trying out different forms of writing, drawing on experience of the models available. May find it difficult to sustain initial efforts over longer pieces of writing. Mainly using language and sentence structures that are close to speech. Spellings of familiar words are generally correct and attempts at unfamiliar spellings reveal a widening range of strategies. Using sentence punctuation more consistently.	2b-a
Moderately experienced writer 3	Shaping writing in familiar genres confidently, drawing on experience of reading. Widening range of writing and taking on different forms more successfully. Aware of audience and beginning to consider appropriateness of language and style. Learning to revise own texts with support and to link and develop ideas coherently. Spellings of words with regular patterns are mainly correct and attempts at unfamiliar words show a growing knowledge of visual patterns and word structures. Using sentence punctuation appropriately.	3
Experienced writer 4	A self-motivated writer who can write at length and is beginning to use writing to refine own ideas. Developing own style and range as a writer but needing support with the structuring of more complex narrative and non-narrative forms. Likely to be reflecting on writing and revising texts for a reader, choosing language for effect or to clarify meanings. Using standard spelling more consistently and drawing on effective self help strategies. Increasingly able to use punctuation, including paragraphing, to organise texts.	4
Exceptionally experienced writer 5	A self-motivated writer who can write at length and is beginning to use writing to refine own ideas. Developing own style and range as a writer but needing support with the structuring of more complex narrative and non-narrative forms. Likely to be reflecting on writing and revising texts for a reader, choosing language for effect or to clarify meanings. Using standard spelling more consistently and drawing on effective self help strategies. Increasingly able to use punctuation, including paragraphing, to organise texts.	5

©CLPE

4

BOYS AND TEACHERS

PRACTICES AND ATTITUDES

At the beginning of the project, the classes involved in the *Promoting Boys' Literacy Learning at Key Stage 2* project were asked "What is literacy?" The point of this question was to gain some insight into children's definitions of literacy and their understanding of what it can include. Here are the answers from two of the classes, in order:

Writing
Spelling
Punctuation
Vocabulary
Talking
Grammar
Stories
    (Teacher K's class)

Writing
Drafting
Editing
Guided reading
Discussions
Spelling
Punctuation
Handwriting
Comprehension
    (Teacher S's class)

Their answers give a fairly clear snapshot of what many of the children think 'literacy' is. According to these pupils 'literacy' seems to be something that happens only in school and is centrally concerned with writing. It was surprising that reading was either low on the lists or unlisted, or appeared only as 'guided reading'. In some classes books were not mentioned at all. These attitudes probably reflect children's experience of the Literacy Hour, but may also reflect a wider pattern of decline in the number of children, especially boys, who read for pleasure (Sainsbury 2003).

Interviews with 24 boys (sixteen in Year 5, eight in Year 4) were carried out at the beginning of the project. The interviews covered their likes and dislikes in literacy, their home literacy, and their experiences of ICT. At the same time, the six teachers were asked to describe their approaches to the teaching of literacy and were invited to suggest explanations for why boys underachieve in literacy.

Name & Age
_____

School & Class
_____

What do you like to read? (favourite authors, texts, websites, computer games; favourite styles such as fantasy, adventure, science fiction, history, stories, comics, magazines, poetry, etc.)

What kinds of writing do you like to do? (stories, plays, letters, bookmaking, poems, email, chat rooms, text messaging, information, diaries, leaflets, posters, etc.)

What is your least favourite reading and writing?

Do you have a computer at home?
Do you read or write on the computer at home?
About how often and for how long do you go on the computer at home?

What do you do on the computer in school?

Are there aspects of reading or writing you find difficult?
What kinds of things help you?

Do you like to talk about what you are reading or writing with friends or with the teacher, or your family?

Do you like working in a group during Literacy? What kinds of literacy work to you do in groups?

Do you have talking time or discussions during Literacy?

What kinds of drama do you do in school?

What is your Mum or Dad reading at the moment?

What are you reading at the moment?

Interviews with boys

Reading

The first surprise was that, contrary to popular views of what boys like to read, not one of the 24 boys interviewed said that he preferred reading information books to reading stories or novels. Boys said they like to read stories and novels about:

Action   *Adventure*
Horror   *Space*
Sport   *Science fiction*

They said they preferred these kinds of books because:
"Of the descriptions"
"You have to find something out"
"It's exciting"
"It's not boring"
"I can imagine myself in them"
"I'm good at sport"
"It makes you want to read more"

Two boys said they liked reading comics because:
"You can get prizes."
"They've got lots of action, lots of art, people, horror – good books, comics."

Although not one boy said he preferred non-fiction or information books to stories and novels, groups of boys in several classes were observed to network around non-fiction texts such as the Dorling Kindersley Eyewitness series, sports magazines and almanacs. During free reading time, for instance, a group of Year 4 boys in School B devised an elaborate and sustained reading and writing game involving a soccer almanac, white boards, pens, and a rotating quizmaster.

Many of these boys expressed sensitivity about their status as readers and writers in the class. When asked about what kinds of reading they disliked, six boys stated: "I hate reading old books". Further questioning revealed that they, as well as other boys, meant not old-fashioned books or books written long ago, but
"Books I used to read when I was little"
"Baby books"
"Books that are too quick"
"Easy books"
"Fast books"
"Picture books"
"Small books"

As Benny in Year 5 wrote in his reading diary:
"I did not like the book it was for babys (sic)."

These boys want to be seen reading 'hard' books, they don't like to be seen reading 'baby' books or books which they or their peers perceive as 'too easy'. At the time of the project, many Year 5s were seen carrying *Lord of the Rings* about, even though they were unable to read it independently. In a silent reading period in Year Five at School C, Christopher chose *Harry Potter and the Chamber of Secrets*, opened the novel on his desk and sat for 20 minutes without turning a page.

Sixteen boys, two-thirds of the case study pool, were on a 'Stage of English' (Hester 1990), a 1-to-5 scale that assesses the needs of children with English as an Additional Language (page 24). However, none of the case study pool was receiving additional language support in school. Two boys were on the ALS programme (Additional Literacy Support, a National Literacy Strategy scheme of work to boost attainment of targeted underachievers). This raised questions about the extent of this group's understanding of literacy tasks and their need for further support. One Year 5 Caribbean Heritage boy (Callan) put it bluntly: "I don't like reading because I don't understand the words and the language." Whilst only two boys were on the ALS programme, eight boys were listed as School Action or School Action Plus (DfES Code of Practice for Special Educational Needs 2002) for challenging behaviour.

Writing

The majority of the 24 boys said they like to write stories because:
"I like to make them up"
"I can use my imagination"
"It doesn't have to be normal, I can put anything in it, it can be MAD, whatever I want"
"You can make up your own words"
"I like writing as a character"
"It makes me feel BIG about myself"
"I can express myself"
"It takes me long and I have loads of ideas"
"It's fun and you can put anything in it"
"I might solve them"
"At home when I'm bored I write stories"

What these boys dislike about writing tends to focus around technical, structural and transcriptional aspects, including:

Spelling   *Handwriting*
Punctuation   *Rewriting*
Beginning a story *Ending a story*

'Getting ideas' and 'not having enough time' were also high on the list of writing difficulties experienced by the boys interviewed. Boys generally assessed their reading abilities as higher than their abilities in writing:

Omar, Year 5: *"I am a pretty good reader but I get stuck writing because I don't know what to say what is going to happen next."*

Zak, Year 5: *"I'm an average reader but my handwriting is not good."*

A few boys expressed frustration about writing stories because of what they saw as the over-long process of drafting, re-drafting and writing:

"I don't like writing stories, it takes too long, you have to think of a title, you have to think of the cover, you write it and write it again, it takes LONG…I like to write poetry and I like listening to poems in the Jamaican language. I like to write poems because a poem you can write in one day, a story takes like ten days."
(Okieriete, Year 4)

Some had quite narrow ideas about what makes a 'good' piece of writing:

"It's hard to get the punctuation just right, because if you want it [the writing] *to be good you got to get loads of description and punctuation – but it's hard to keep having it running through the whole story."*
(Jermaine, Year 5)

For some boys, reading is something over which they can exercise choice and control, while writing is inevitably assigned and controlled by the teacher.

"I hate writing poetry and I hate writing diaries where you are supposed to be a character. I hate writing reports and newspaper stories and plays. I don't like writing stories but I like to read stories. I read for three hours if it's something that I'm interested in. Even five hours."
(Danny, Year 5)

Family patterns of literacy

23 of the 24 boys said it was their mothers who helped with their homework; one boy said his father helped him because his mother, who is Somali, has no English. Boys also reported their mothers as being engaged in a range of reading, including:

Magazines
Newspapers
Library books
"Books about stress"
Harry Potter
The Bible
The Koran
College books
Homework for nursing, midwifery and accounting qualifications

But they typically reported about their fathers:

"My dad, he just works, I don't see him read."
(Jason, Year 5)

Using computers at home

21 out of the 24 boys reported having a computer at home, which they use between one and three hours every day for

writing letters and stories
using art programmes such as 'Paint'
word processing homework (Year 5s only)
surfing the internet
going to websites
playing games

Boys who have home computers use them overwhelmingly for playing games and visiting a wide range of websites mainly for entertainment, but also to look at authors' pages and educational sites such as the BBC's Revisewise, Megamaths, and Spycatcher.

- *(Benny, Year 5) "I go on it every night, as long as I can. I go on Foxkids, Nickleodeon, Cartoon Network, Shockwave, and I look at trailers for movies."*

- *(Jason, Year 5) "The games I like are violent games, shooting and racing."*

- *(Kenneth, Year 5) "I go on for as long as I can, until my sister kicks me off so she can do her college work."*

- *(Danny, Year 5) "Right now I'm reading on the [author] Darren Shan website. My mother also showed me BBC Revisewise and sometimes I do work on that."*

Although they may claim that their fathers don't read, the home computer is where many of these boys and their fathers are engaging together in literacy. The 21 boys with home computers reported playing on the computer with their fathers, and also with older brothers or sisters.

- *(K, Year 5) "My dad and me play on the computer, we look at websites."*
- *(C, year 5) "My dad makes his own computer games."*
- *(K, Year 5) "My dad is an ICT teacher and knows all about that. He tells me what's good"*
- *(B, Year 5) "We look at movie trailers to see if we want to go or not."*
- *(J, Year 5) "We play the Shockwave games."*

The amount of computer use by boys was an unexpected finding, and interviews with teachers often revealed their different attitudes to and knowledge about ICT. Boys identified as underachieving were often articulate about their preferences, strengths and weaknesses in school literacy, but their strategies for learning were not always school-based. As Omar said about his writing: "What I do when I get stuck is I think of a TV programme."

Interviews with teachers

Poor behaviour

The view that boys' behaviour is the root cause of their underachievement predominated in teacher interviews. Teachers gave as the reasons for boys' underachievement in literacy:

> *Poor behaviour (5 teachers)*
> *Playground fighting (3 teachers)*
> *Can't sit still (4 teachers)*
> *Lack of concentration (4 teachers)*
> *They can't think for themselves (1 teacher)*
> *They can't work independently (1 teacher)*
> *Reading and writing is un-cool (2 teachers)*
> *The range of resources still favours girls (1 teacher)*
> *Physical immaturity (1 teacher)*

Teachers were often pessimistic about boys' ability in literacy:

Teacher K: "*They're fussy, fickle readers. I have to be so sensitive about what I suggest for them to read. They can't write independently. We don't send home books and reading diaries because boys never bring them back. Boys don't read at home, no matter how many rewards and stars we offer. Parents don't read to them, they're too busy working.*"

Teacher S: "*They are unable to structure a coherent story, no matter how many frames and plans I give them. I'm at my wit's end about it. They never take it seriously.*"

Teacher P: "*There's a group and they have a bad influence on each other. But I put them together, because why should all the others suffer?*"

Teacher G: "*Writing is physically difficult for them, a real effort.*"

Teacher L: "*They have no independent strategies for writing. Without constant scaffolding at every step they totally fall apart. They don't take it seriously, they get silly.*"

Teacher J: "*They don't show any imagination. They can't think for themselves.*"

Following the interviews, teachers were asked to evaluate their whole class using Gemma Moss' (1999) categories of

1) children who are 'can and do' readers and writers, who read and write freely and in a self-motivated way

2) children who are 'can but don't' readers and writers, who are technically capable but who don't voluntarily choose to read and write and may avoid literacy tasks

can and do mostly girls, some boys	**can but don't** only boys
can't and don't mostly boys, some girls	**can't but try** mostly girls, some boys

with thanks to Gemma Moss, The Fact & Fiction Project (1999)

3) children who are 'can't and don't' readers and writers, who cannot yet read and write independently and don't choose to

To this was added a fourth category –

4) children who 'can't - but do try.' These are children who cannot yet read and write independently but will attempt reading and writing tasks

Teachers identified both boys and girls in categories 1, 3 and 4 – but placed only boys in category 2: 'can but don't'. *No teacher identified any girl as a 'can-but-don't' reader or writer.* Instead they attributed girls' underachievement to particular learning difficulties (eg. dyslexia, English as an additional language) and viewed underachieving girls as making an effort ('can't

Boys' Achievement Project Teacher Questionnaire

Name

LEA

School

Year Group

How many years teaching, which year groups?

School role/subject coordinator:

Reading & Writing

Tell me what ideas you have developed, from your own observation and record-keeping, about factors affecting boys' achievement in literacy?

There is a recognised gap in test scores for reading and scores for writing, much more so for boys than for girls. What have you noticed about:
- the amount of reading boys do
- the kinds of texts they choose
- their willingness to write or their enjoyment of writing
- the things they write about
- the reading-writing gap

Can you tell me what kinds of reading and writing you think boys like best? Worst? Why do you think this is? Any gender differences here?

What do you know about boys' reading or writing at home? Do you think this may be very different from their school literacy?

How many whole texts have you used for literacy this year (not including story or novel you read to class at the end of the day?)

Some teachers have noticed in boys an inability to write coherently at length – what is your observation about this?

Do boys ever say anything about their reading or writing that surprises you?

Professional issues

Are there things you would like to be doing in your teaching but feel unable to due to timetable or other curriculum constraints?

Are there particular school policies that you think are effective in promoting boys' literacy achievement? (eg: male mentors, home-school liaison)

What do you feel are your most successful teaching strategies for raising boys' achievement?

Do you have any concerns about focusing on boys at the expense of girls?

Many people point to the lack of male role models in primary school – how do you feel about this?

What is your view of the Literacy Hour/NLS? How strictly do you stick to it?

What kinds of literacy happen in your classroom outside the Literacy Hour?

Talk

Tell me what kind of language or discussion activities you think support or promote reading and writing? (eg: reading aloud, children reading aloud, performance readings, extended whole class book discussions, writing response partners?)

Had you heard of Aidan Chamber's 'Tell Me' Questions and 'Book Talk' before the INSET?

How often do you do these things with your class (Daily, Weekly, 2-3 times per week, once a term, never?):
- Book Talk
- Read aloud to class
- Children reading each other's writing aloud or in writing conferences
- Drama
- Children performance readings
- Children's collaborative reading or writing

In your class, what kinds of literacy activities involve children talking? What outcomes do you plan from these discussions?

Can you describe how you group children for literacy? What is the purpose of the groupings?

Do you have any Literacy Hour group work (teacher-led or independent) that involves talking?

Do you plan for talk as part of your literacy planning?

Do you keep any records for talk?

Tell me what are you currently planning for drama and role play?

Social contexts of learning

Could you tell me if you organise any of these activities and about how often (daily/weekly/once or twice termly/never) – please indicate:

	Pair	Small group	Group with adult	Whole class
Collaborative reading activities				
Collaborative writing activities				
Drama and role play activities				
Problem solving talk/brainstorming				
ICT activities for literacy				

ICT (attitudes, skills, provision)

There is some research that suggests boys use ICT in very different ways at home compared to school – what do you know about boys' use of ICT at home? Do you notice gender differences around ICT in school?

What kinds of ICT activities do you plan linked to literacy?

Tell me what you think is the role of ICT in literacy.

Would you say you plan for ICT in literacy on a daily or a weekly basis? Or less than that?

Is it mainly in class or mainly in an ICT suite?

Tell me what kinds of opportunities children have to use ICT in their literacy work?

Are there skills you would like to develop in ICT that you think would affect the way you teach reading and writing?

but do try') in spite of their difficulties. Several boys were identified as 'can and do readers', but as 'can but don't' writers. The majority of boys in the focus group were identified as 'can-but-don't' readers and writers.

'can and do' readers and writers	'can but don't' readers and writers
Adnan	Michael Jamel Benny Christopher
Dapo	Omar Kerwin Yusuf Kenneth
Zak	Alhassan Melvin Samil Kwaku
	read but don't write
	Danny Aaron
can't and don't read and write	**can't read or write but tries**
Okieriete Ashley Victor Ali	Wilfred Jermaine James

Teachers often identified clear styles, patterns and preferences in boys' learning, but tended to view these as unhelpful:

 Teacher P: *"They talk for England. They talk forever but it never makes it to the page."*

 Teacher J: *"They have to find out what their friends are writing first."*

 Teacher K: *"They love to share their stories – especially without the teacher being there! ... They love talking about their ideas and discussing them and then once I say, right, can we get this onto paper, they don't enjoy that as much as they do talking about it."*

Teacher G: *"They may not read books but they read other things: CDs, lyrics, manuals, websites"*

Teacher J: *"They like football, sports, it's got to be exciting for them."*

Using ICT

Four of the six teachers agreed with the statement: *'boys know more about computers than I do'*. One said knowledge was *'about equal now'* and one (an ICT co-ordinator) disagreed with the statement. Two teachers used their class computers regularly for literacy, using a range of CD ROMs for literacy and maths drills or linked to history and geography topics. Teacher L organized daily access to the class computer and each child had an ICT diary to mark their progress across a range of tasks. Teacher P routinely deployed laptops around the classroom, in addition to the class computer, for a range of tasks in history or science and for independent writing; at the end of the project year

children in this class were creating their own multi-media texts. All classes had access to a computer suite once a week (although in one school this access was once a week every other half term) to work through ICT schemes of work.

All six teachers acknowleged that boys would like to use the computer more often, but some teachers felt unsure about managing boys' learning on computers.

Teacher S: *"I'm never sure exactly what they're doing, what they are learning, when they are on the computer, they go clicking and navigating and they go off-task. I would use the class computer more, but I'm not sure how to make it fair so that everyone gets a chance."*

Teacher G: *"They would stay on the computer all day if I let them. Personally, I don't use it that much. I know it's covered in papers right now."*

Teacher K: *"They would do anything to get on it. They are obsessed by the computer. They get too noisy and over-excited on the computer."*

Teachers were on the whole uninterested in the cyber-culture that boys reported engaging with at home;

Teacher J: *"I don't know that much about it. I think other things are more important. A lot of it is very stupid and violent. I feel school should offer something different."*

Teacher S: *"There must be lots of really good, interesting websites they would like but I don't know what they are."*

Teacher L was an exception: *"A year ago I had never touched a computer. Now I use it for everything."*

Curriculum constraints

Project teachers had uneven knowledge about literacy as pedagogy. None had heard of Genre Theory, a key influence on the National Literacy Strategy; three had heard of Aidan Chambers' *Tell Me* (Chambers 1993) (the basis of one of the intervention approaches). Four teachers felt under pressure to cover all the NLS objectives, and sometimes felt constrained in their planning by the school and their colleagues:

Teacher S: *"With the Literacy Strategy, you can never get carried away, you're always aware that you have to be moving on to the next thing."*

Teacher L: "*I read all about [Chambers] Book Talk in college, but when I got here and began planning as part of a team it became difficult – especially since I was new. I wanted to do poetry and they said – what again?*"

All six teachers read regularly from a class novel as an end-of-the-day winding down, pleasurable activity. However only two teachers regularly taught literacy using whole texts (ie not through extracts), and only two routinely used drama approaches to literacy. Before the project began, only one teacher had routinely planned for talk as a literacy activity. Three teachers grouped children by ability for literacy (two in Year 5, one in Year 4) and three teachers organised mixed-ability groups for literacy (two in Year 5, one in Year 4).

These initial interviews often revealed significant differences between the attitudes and practices of teachers and the attitudes and practices of boys, particularly in the area of ICT. It was also striking that most of the boys said they *liked* reading and writing stories, and that they liked using their imaginations for writing. Since they said they enjoy these activities, why was their achievement in writing so poor? Teachers believed boys' behaviour to be the main reason for their underachievement in literacy - what kinds of texts and teaching would successfully engage boys in literacy learning?

Over two terms, the *Promoting Boys' Literacy Learning at Key Stage 2* project would develop and evaluate interventions designed to bridge these gaps. CLPE asked teachers to adopt some specific teaching approaches: to teach literacy from whole texts, to engage children in forms of oral rehearsal (discussion, collaboration, role playenactment), to use text-based ICT for discussion, reading and writing, and to create different types of audiences for children's writing. As the interventions were introduced, this research looked not only at boys' learning and behaviour but also at how teachers' planning, and the different 'teaching sequences' they developed (outlined below), reflected their interpretations of the interventions.

Teaching Sequences: 'What Has Happened to Lulu'

Year 4 teaching sequence: poetry focus
- reading & re-reading, reading aloud
- memorizing & getting the 'rhythm' of the poem
- visualising and drawing Lulu's room and house
- writing Lulu's note
- emails to Lulu & to author Charles Causley (resulting in emails to characters in other texts such as The Highwayman and Willy the Wimp)
- role play: mother-Lulu discussion
- looking closely at the form of the stanzas (questions, repetition)
- discussion of what makes a poem a poem, reading favourite poems
- writing own Lulu stanza (draft and re-write)
- big book created of collected notes, stanzas, emails and drawings
- display of crumpled notes on a 'fire'

Year 5 teaching sequence: drama, talk and "play" writing focus
- reading, discussion
- notes in role from Lulu
- role play, thought tracking: what Mum is thinking
- freeze-framing scenes from each stanza; writing each stanza as a mini-play
- exchange of texts and emails in role (no actual computer use)
- closure discussion and role play (Lulu returns home)

Year 5 teaching sequence: writing focus
- reading and discussion
- Lulu interactive software in computer suite and in class
- writing letters and notes in role - adding visual elements (blood stains, crumpled notes)
- emails to Lulu
- adding to CBBC discussion board about runaways
- writing description of Lulu's room (draft and re-write)
- letters to author Charles Causley (draft and re-write)
- display of "Lulu's Room" writing in class

Teaching Sequences: *The Seal Wife*

Year 4 teaching sequence: Collaborative writing focus
- reading, re-reading and 'book talk'
- looking for pictures, artwork of mermaids in and out of school
- developing the 'pleading' scene individually and bringing together as playscript dialogues
- collaborative drafting and writing continuations of the story: the fate of the seal children
- performance readings of story continuations
- reading more Causley poems about the sea
- watercolour paintings, sea colours
- collaborative texts printed on seascape watercolour paintings and displayed

Year 5 teaching sequence: independent writing focus
- reading aloud to class, book talk,
- visualisation followed by writing introductory paragraph
- drawings of beach scene
- mind-mapping plans
- reading and discussing software in computer suite
- discussion prompts in literacy groups
- drafting and writing seal stories in chapters, editing prompts with partner
- using ICT to design book cover and blurb
- read stories to reception children, ask them 'book talk' questions
- web publishing

Year 5 teaching sequence: performance reading focus
- read and discuss story; two versions
- guided reading using software, discussion
- small group discussion and collaborative drafting of each character's perspective (seal wife, husband, children); each perspective read and reflected upon by whole class
- individual writing of perspectives and arguments from group draft ideas; draft and final copy
- performance readings: The Seal Wife in Divorce Court

5

PEDAGOGIES AND PLANNING

INTRODUCING AND MANAGING ORACY

This section of *Boys on the Margin* describes the teaching approaches promoted by the project and adopted by the teachers involved. These planned interventions all involved oral and interactive approaches to literacy. However, before embarking on some of these interventions, it seemed important to respond to some of the management issues involved in planning for talk in the classroom. Our first intervention, based on the work of Dawes et al (2000) was therefore aimed at establishing some ground rules for talk which would facilitate the use of oral and interactive approaches in children's learning.

Neil Mercer's work recognises that children may not have enough experience of using talk in their learning to appreciate what is expected of them in class or group discussion and may need to be explicitly inducted into these more formal ways of talking which enable larger groups to work together. His ideas are developed in his work *Thinking Together* (Dawes, Mercer & Wegerif, 2000) and were shared with project teachers.

Exploratory talk occurs when partners engage critically but constructively with each other's ideas. Relevant knowledge is shared, suggestions are sought and opinions are offered for joint consideration. ...In exploratory talk, knowledge is made publicly accountable and reasoning becomes apparent in the talk. ...The ability to use language in this way is a valuable part of children's education – in adult life they will need to be able to use it effectively in work situations and in order to take an active role in society. (p 4)

Children may never have thought about how they talk together or considered whether different ways of communicating might make group activities more productive and enjoyable. They need help to learn how to use language effectively. As teachers, we may not have made our expectations sufficiently clear when we ask pupils to 'discuss' or 'talk together in a group'. (p 5)

Rules for Talk

At the beginning of the project, these approaches were formally introduced to each class by the project officer. She invited the classes to develop 'rules for talk' with their teachers. These ideas were then posted on the project website and made into posters or cards for the classroom. Children participated enthusiastically in these discussions and generated very positive sets of 'rules'. Part of the discussion involved deciding how and when these rules would be referred to.

Talk Rules by Year 5
We Try Our Best To Carry These Out
1. We take turns to speak
2. We listen to each other
3. We look at the person talking
4. We respect each other and are polite
5. We may need to agree to disagree!
   We do this politely
6. We speak calmly and quietly and don't shout
7. We ask questions to encourage and show we have listened

Rules for Discussions by Year 4
- If someone says something wrong or makes a mistake we try not to laugh. We treat each other with respect.
- We may disagree at times but explain why in a polite way.
- Think before we ask questions or express an opinion.
- We can try to reach an agreement.
- Listen to whoever is talking.
- Discuss things together and ask everyone for their opinion.
- Give everyone time to express their ideas.
- Try not to interrupt because it distracts their ideas, flow and concentration.
- Please Read Me At Least Once A Week.

Year 5's Rules for Talking and Discussion
- Think about what you say.
- Listen to each other.
- Share your ideas.
- Cooperate with your group.
- Make sure everyone has a chance to speak. Take turns.
- Agree to disagree.
- Work as a team.
- Respond to what others say.
- Talk quietly, don't shout.

Teachers found these ideas helpful in class behaviour management but not all were sure of their application to literacy teaching. The results tended to be circular: those classes which engaged in extended group and whole class discussions would refer to the rules more often than those classes which engaged in more limited forms of talk. In one class, the rules were posted high up on a wall and were difficult to read; in another class, the rules were on a dozen laminated cards in the book area, for easy reference.

Teachers' introduction and management of oral work varied considerably, with some teachers maintaining more control over the content and the direction of children's talk. Three teachers (Teachers S,K &L) organised 'Talk Tables' for Literacy. Teacher L organized single sex tables for talk and reported that "it took nerves of steel" but that over time results were positive as boys began to call on shared experiences for discussion and to share, compare and network around texts, particularly in the Summer term when they were reading the Louis Sachar novel. Two teachers (Teachers S and K) prepared written talk prompts to guide independent group discussions; others (Teachers L, G, P) would direct children to discuss issues, make collaborative notes and report back to the class.

Book Talk

The second intervention made by the project related to talk about texts. We drew on the long-term experience of advisory staff at CLPE who had regularly made extensive use of Aidan Chambers' approaches to discussion, which are described in *Tell Me: Children, Reading and Talk* (1993). In this book Chambers describes ways in which classes can learn to talk about books together, drawing on all the resources of the group:

In Book Talk we all, as a community of readers, cooperate to draw out of each other what we think we know about a text and our reading of it. (ibid:75).

Teachers were introduced to this approach in an INSET session and discussed how they could apply it in their classrooms. Some teachers were already familiar with Chambers basic Book Talk questions:

- Was there anything that you liked about this book?
- Was there anything that you disliked?

- Was there anything that puzzled you?
- Were there any patterns – any connections – that you noticed?

Teacher G was already using Book Talk in guided reading groups as well as with the whole class, and used guided reading "as a time for discussion, finding out what they think about the book, not just hearing each one read around a circle."

Those teachers who did not have experience teaching from whole texts were more unsure about how and when to use Chambers' basic 'Tell Me' questions and how to conduct Book Talk. Teacher S gave 'Tell Me' questions to the school Learning Support Assistants who read individually with pupils, as a way of enhancing that interaction. In the course of the project some teachers became more confident about conducting Book Talk with large groups. They found that the 'Tell Me' approach, which invites children to share their responses, helped to engage the class more fully and to generate more extensive discussion around texts.

Drama

The project foregrounded drama as part of the oral and interactive approaches to literacy that it was promoting. We referred back to a previous CLPE research project, published as *The Reader in the Writer* (Barrs and Cork 2001), for evidence that drama could provide a strikingly immediate route into a fictional situation. We were convinced that drama was a way of learning which was accessible and involving for children. We therefore promoted the use of drama as a way of exploring some of the texts introduced in the course of the project.

In *The Reader in the Writer*, Susanna Steele and Fiona Collins (page 222) write about learning through drama and observe:

The triggering of an affective response is essential to the study of literature and it can be elusive for many children when the text is approached only in formal ways.

We hoped that the use of more active and enactive approaches to texts would enable children to enter the world of a text more fully. As part of the preparation for this aspect of the work, we invited Susanna Steele of Greenwich University to conduct a drama and planning workshop for the project teachers during the first INSET. Using one of the intervention texts, the Charles Causley poem *What Has Happened to Lulu?*, teachers developed a range of dramatic responses, which included visualising and 'walking around' Lulu's room, 'freeze-framing' a tableau from the poem, enacting each stanza as a mini-play, and putting the drama on paper through different forms of writing.

Drama was an area where teachers varied considerably in their experience and in comfort levels. Two teachers had used role play and drama for literacy in the past, other teachers were sticking their toes in the water for the first time. It was important that teachers used drama in ways that were comfortable for them, and they developed different techniques for managing drama. Teacher P did this by taking a strong participatory and managerial role in drama sessions. For Teacher L, teaching children about 'freeze framing' a moment in their enactment of a text was effective as a way of maintaining control and focus. Teacher K would involve one or two children in 'thought-tracking', or thinking aloud in role as one of the characters, with the rest of the class taking the role of questioners. Teacher G's class would write informal notes about the language, descriptions and feelings that had emerged during their role play, and would build upon these in subsequent writing.

Planning and assessment

Developing units of work which included discussion and drama around whole texts often involved considerable class work outside the Literacy Hour, (DfEE 1998) particularly to make time for a good range of writing. Teacher P was unrepentant about the extended time that children spent on a single text, remarking: "It's criminal to stop them when they're on a roll." Over the course of two terms, units of work were developed which took place both in and outside of the Literacy Hour:

Outside the Literacy Hour:
- (Teacher K) 'Talk tables' for literacy, drama sessions
- (Teacher S) Emailing book characters
- (Teacher J) Writing workshops
- (Teacher L) Daily writing time, drama and performance
- (Teacher G) Discussion, drama, reading, writing
- (Teacher P) Extended writing

Inside the Literacy Hour
- (Teacher K) Word work, spelling and handwriting
- (Teacher S) Word & sentence work, guided reading and independent groups
- (Teacher J) Shared reading, guided reading, independent work
- (Teacher L) Word and sentence work
- (Teacher G) Sentence work, handwriting
- (Teacher P) Shared reading, independent writing

The amount of time teachers devoted to the interventions varied according to what they felt they could take on, working within the parameters dictated by their school, their year group and the literacy curriculum. One teacher opted out of her school's planning to carry out the interventions. For the three teachers who did not strictly follow the NLS, the interventions were easily integrated into their medium term plans. For two teachers, the interventions were carried out in addition to their school and year group literacy plans.

Some teachers felt unclear about the learning outcomes of the interventions involving oracy, because drama, speaking and listening often have no immediate, 'markable' outcomes. Whilst teachers felt secure in assessing reading and writing, they often felt less sure about how to assess oral work and drama in their own right, although two teachers kept records of children's oral work using the Primary Language Record (CLPE 1996).

Teachers found that oral approaches to literacy demand a focus on the whole text, rather than on the 'parts' of 'literacy' (as described by children at the beginning of Chapter Four), and for some teachers this was a departure from how they had been organizing the teaching of literacy. However, as some teachers already knew and other teachers discovered, a focus on the whole text does generate its own word and sentence level work. Most importantly, these oral approaches to a text led to literacy work which in some cases, and especially for the boys whose learning we focused on, was a significant advance on what they had done before.

6

TEXTS AND INTERACTION

This section of *Boys on the Margin* focuses on the teaching and learning that took place during and after reading, and before, during and after writing. In these pedagogic spaces, children experienced, internalised and responded to their reading. They made texts they had read or heard meaningful to themselves. They responded to texts in discussions and through the creation of their own written texts. Teachers involved in the project aimed to make these processes, in which children moved between reading and writing and from reading to writing, more comprehensible and more engaging through the regular use of talk and interactive approaches.

Over two terms, project teachers introduced a poem, a short story and a novel to their classes. They orchestrated talk, the use of ICT, and drama around each text to develop a range of writing. In this project, it is the boys' reading, writing and talk that are being highlighted, but it is important to remember that boys were often reading, writing and talking with girls, who also brought their experiences and responses to discussions and to drama.

What Has Happened to Lulu?

Drama on paper

What Has Happened to Lulu is a poem that lends itself readily to Book Talk. It is a mysterious poem, spoken in the voice of a younger child (possibly Lulu's sister or brother). The poem consists of a series of questions addressed to the child's mother, which build up an atmosphere of anxiety and foreboding. In the course of the poem some of the circumstances of Lulu's disappearance in the night emerge, and we can begin to imagine possible scenarios. This poem is a kind of drama on paper, the research team wanted to foreground this in the interventions.

This is a poem which CLPE teaching staff had used successfully in the past in INSET, workshops and ICT courses. For the purposes of the project we developed further ICT-related activities around the poem. As well as the discussion and drama approaches developed in Susanna Steele's INSET therefore (page 38), teachers made use of interactive ICT to help children develop their language and ideas before writing in response to the poem. Unexpectedly, email emerged

as a significant area of imaginative writing for boys, as they enthusiastically entered the fictional world of a girl who seems to have run away from home.

What Has Happened to Lulu?

What has happened to Lulu, mother?
   What has happened to Lu?
There's nothing in her bed but an old rag doll
   And by its side, a shoe.

Why is her window wide, mother,
   The curtain flapping free,
And only a circle on the dusty shelf
   Where her money box used to be?

Why do you turn your head, mother,
   And why do the tear-drops fall?
And why do you crumple that note on the fire
   And say it is nothing at all?

I woke to voices late last night,
   I heard an engine roar.
Why do you tell me the things I heard
   Were a dream and nothing more?

I heard somebody cry, mother,
   In anger or in pain,
But now I ask you why, mother,
   You say it was a gust of rain.

Why do you wander about as though
   You don't know what to do?
What has happened to Lulu, mother?
   What has happened to Lu?

(Charles Causley, 1917 – 2003)

Children's interpretations

Some teachers who were less experienced in using poetry and drama were unsure at the outset about using the Charles Causley poem. They expressed reservations:

"I don't do a lot of poetry"
"We just finished a unit on poetry"
"Poetry – it's not me"
"My class won't understand this poem"
"Boys won't like this poem, it's very old-fashioned"
"I don't do a lot of drama"

This deceptively simple text however did generate intense discussion in the project classes. What *did* happen to Lulu? What did she write in the note that the mother threw on the fire? Where did she go? Why did she leave? In Book Talk sessions, teachers encouraged children to visualize the world of the poem, to 'walk around Lulu's room' and generate ideas about who is speaking in the poem, who the characters are, and what their relationships are like. These comments show a Year 4 class in the process of working out these details from the text:

Teacher G: (Where is this poem taking place?)
"I think this is taking place in an old house in the living room, they are meeting up in the living room because it is a good place to meet up."
"I think it's a haunted house because the haunted house is dusty."
"I think it's in a cottage because I can imagine it old and dusty and misty"
"In a dirty place in a farm house"
"I think the house is a spooky house"

(Who is Lulu? How old is she?)
"The bigger sister because the little sister is asking the mother, where is she?"
"She has been taken away"
"Some one who has disappeared, a girl or boy lodger"
"A girl, a daughter"
"A big girl, because as a teenager they forget how much their parents love them"
"A teenager, because she has an OLD rag doll"
"Very young because of her name"
"Eleven, because she left her things on the floor"
"Fourteen, she ran away with her money"
"Fourteen, she climbed out the window, you will never see her again, she is old enough to go by herself."

Discussions about this poem in project classes touched on many sensitive issues such as domestic violence, foster homes, runaways, drugs, kidnapping and murder. The ideas that children like these Year 4s brought to the text were not easy or comfortable:

"She might have been kidnapped by a robber"
"She might have gone to stay with her friend"
"Or maybe even she might have been murdered, or ran away"
"She could have committed suicide"

"She could have been adopted"
"Or she might have found some foster parents"
"Drug dealers broke into her house, took her money and took her away too"
"Maybe she was offered drugs and became a drug addict"
"She ran away because her mother wouldn't let her party"
"Her step-dad was beating her"

Although some teachers had seen the poem as old-fashioned and likely to be uninteresting to modern children, many children interpreted the poem in a completely contemporary way. Using their own experiences, or what they knew from television and other media, they updated the poem without any input or prompting.

Dramatic interaction: walking around Lulu's room

Teacher K's class developed a series of physical, visual and verbal interactions from the text, in which small groups of children enacted each stanza of the poem as a mini-play, giving each line a voice, an action and an emotion. Children had to imagine the speakers, their roles, genders and ages, where they would be, in which room, and what they might be doing as they spoke. This was a first step for some boys in acting-out a piece of writing within a thought-out context and with a purpose:

(Mum, Lauren and Danny in the front room. Mum stands in front of the fire reading the letter. Danny and Lauren stand next to Mum)
Lauren: *(in a tearful voice) Why do you turn your head, Mother, why do the teardrops fall?*
(Mum throws the note on the fire)

Danny: *(sadly) And why do you crumple that note on the fire? (Playscript by Danny, Lauren & Rammone)*

In the silent - but central - role of 'Mum', Rammone dramatically threw the note on an imaginary fire, covered his face with his hands and pretended to weep. Rammone was engaged in this enactment of the poem, and it gave him an idea for writing an imaginary email from the mother to Lulu:

To: Lulu20@hotmail.com
Subject: I have got all the money and you ante got none so ante you going to come back I dont want you to come back

Rammone is a 'can't and don't' reader and writer, and he has painted himself into a corner in Year 5: everything he writes is wrong. He dislikes writing and avoids it because it only generates errors to correct.

However, what is interesting in his very short piece of writing is his attention to the *form* of email: to the address and the subject heading. He seems to know a lot about this particular type of writing, and he was able to begin to transfer the drama of the poem onto paper in his own writing.

Enactment gave Rammone an opening to get involved in school literacy. Other can't-and-don't boys became similarly engaged in literacy through this approach to the poem, in which they were not required to write anything. Their first steps before writing would be to speak the text or simply 'be' in the drama as the wordless mother or another character.

In Teacher L's class, groups silently enacted and extended scenes from the poem through mime and tableaux: the discovery and reading of the note, Lulu jumping into a waiting car, the search for Lulu and Lulu returning home. Teacher L noticed that these opportunities to enact the text themselves generated bursts of writing as children planned what they would do: "During discussions leading up to drama, there was a lot of spontaneous writing, on scraps of paper and on white boards"

Drama on paper

Moving from enactment to writing, children quickly scribbled what they thought might be in Lulu's note and then 'crumpled' the message as described in the poem.

Teacher L: "*After the drama, there was an intense period of writing, very short and silent. I didn't even ask for silence, all I said to them was: remember. this is a note that made your mother cry. We didn't have the usual arguments about spellings, pens, pencils, which paper.*"

Omar, in Year 5 in School A, was born in Sierra Leone and came to the UK age 4. At the start of the project, he was at Level 2 for reading and writing in National Curriculum assessments. He speaks Kriol at home, and uses his home computer for 'painting' and writing letters. He also revealed that "when I'm bored I write stories." 'Lulu' inspired him to bring his home writing to school, which he had not done before.

After Teacher S introduced the poem, the following day and without prompting, Omar brought to school this note, which he had word-processed at home:

Dear Mum,
I am writing to say sorry for walking out the house, but you pushed me too far. You know if you didn't have said those things I would be with you and you can keep the old rag doll.
I never wanted this to happen. I'm leaving. Dad, you can come and visit me, I love you .But you should have given me some air. I used the car but that's not the problem, you are. You can't just hit me. Love from Lulu

When he brought this note to school, Teacher S said that she would photocopy it, and Omar replied – "Can't we scan it?".

Teacher S continued this exchange of messages between Lulu and her mother in class. Omar wrote an email (although it was actually handwritten on paper) and a reply. In these brief sketches, he builds a complex picture of a family, of relationships gone bad, an impending marriage, violence, anger and regret.

Email

To: Lulu

Where are you? I want you to come home please. Emma is so sad. Can you find it in your heart to forgive me. Can we be a family? I promise I will be better. Your dad wants you to know that grandma has a heart problem so please don't think about me, think about your 2 sisters, dad, grandma and grandad. I know the way I kept you in like a slave is bad but please with all my heart come home. I'm sorry Lulu, I never meant to hurt you. I never meant to make you cry but tonight I am very sad.
Love Mother

Letter from Lulu

Dear Mother,

I am writing to say how good it is without you. Did you see the note? Mum you pushed me too far. I wish you were normal like other mums, you should always be caring. How is Emma doing? She should come and see Dad and me, that's where I am staying. He likes the fact of me getting married and Dad doesn't hit me. You know I never wanted this

to happen. The thing is you should have given me air to have fun. I love you, I will always. It's just the hitting and arguing, I can't stand it. I used the car yesterday but that's not the problem, you are. You can't keep on hitting me. You will not because I'm not coming back.
Love from Lulu

Teacher S's class performed the poem and their writing to a whole school and parent assembly, where they also performed 'freeze frames' or tableaux of different 'scenes' from the stanzas. Omar's original letter, along with other writing, was published on the project website. These performances and presentations to different audiences, in school and in cyberspace, gave children's writing a clear purpose. In this context, Omar's progress in the National Curriculum was marked; in the course of two terms he was assessed as having made significant progress both in reading and in writing:

Omar	January	July
NC reading	2a	3b
NC writing	2b	3b

Teacher P's Year 5 class created a different kind of drama on paper in response to the Causley poem. Children added visual elements to their writing by daubing Lulu's 'note' with 'bloodstains', and drawing maps of kidnapping and ransom scenarios. Children relished these opportunities to enhance their writing with graphic drawing and decoration.

Dear

Mum and uttle brother I have vanished from me because the educatain is very poor and the people there are Nearly bad but most of them are poor biles exept one of them this one person is my freind and he are is very confidendt to. Work little brother incase you are wondering are. What has happened to me nothing has so you can stop wondering about me. Mum incase you didn's know were I am Iam In the U.S and Wen are having a absouloutly thraung time the educatoin is fabulaus and my freinds mum gives me enough to go to school with very soon mum I will send ttyou leotves of the U.S.

Yours faithfuly

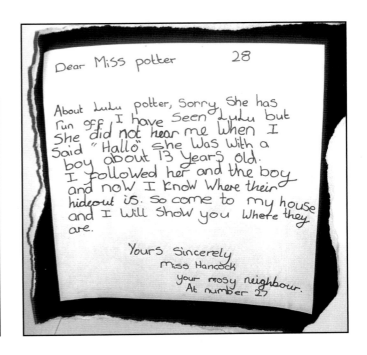

Dear Miss potter   28

About Lulu potter, sorry she has run off. I have seen Lulu but she did not hear me when I said "Hallo" she was with a boy about 13 years old. I followed her and the boy and now I know where their hideout is. So come to my house and I will show you where they are.

Yours Sincerely
miss Hancock
your nosy neighbour.
At number 27

Murder Story at home

The room is pink but smells of murder Lulu has two windows and one smells of DEATH the other one shines with daylight Lulu is sitting and making a note for her mum The handle of her window is mainly covered in blood. Half the ragdolls body and head are missing A bit of Lulu's dress ripped and is on the floor. She has lost her shoe. H window is wide and her curtain flapping because the murderer came in that way. I herd voice and the roar of the undertaker's car and his voice too. Lulu's dead my darling and there is nothing we can do "said my mum "Why do you hang your head in shame and say it was a gust of rain?" I replied.

Some teachers were reluctant to allow children to get carried away with the imagined violence of the poem, and would attempt to turn children's discussions away from issues of drug abuse and domestic violence. Some teachers felt that the issues children raised in 'Lulu' discussions might be more suited to PSHE than Literacy. Yet it was often these 'taboo' topics that motivated focus boys to write enthusiastically.

Formal work

Although writing in role was a major outcome of this intervention, more formal word and sentence work also flowed organically from the study of the poem. Teacher K, for example, devised weekly spelling lists from the poem: anger, pain, voices, roar.

Ali, in Teacher G's Year 4 class, was the only one of 24 boys who said that it was his father rather than his mother who helped him with his homework. His home language is Somali, and he struggles with spelling and handwriting in English. Working with Teacher G, as he talked and looked in a thesaurus, he searched for the right language to write Lulu's note.

Dear mum,
I feel depressed and heartbroken because you treat
me like a baby and you make me go to bed at 8pm.
I am gone with dad. I left in a rush because it was
nearly morning and you would of woke me up for
school. I grew out of my rag doll Elise. If you love
me, write back and put some money.
Love from Lulu (Actually by the magnificent Ali)

There is more here than meets the eye. Although Ali's text is brief, it covers quite a bit of narrative territory. He explains why she left, with whom, and when. He puts readers into Lulu's thoughts and emotions by carefully selecting the charged adjectives *depressed* and *heartbroken*. He lets readers know that she has grown too old for her dolls and is in need of financial help. We find out quite a lot about Lulu from this short piece of writing.

Teacher G's class also read other poems by Charles Causley and scrutinised the form of 'Lulu', with its repeating questions and vocabulary. Afterwards children attempted to write their own stanza for the poem. Ashley is on the Special Needs register as 'School Action' for behaviour and he has Additional Literacy Support ('ALS'). He wrote this new stanza, in the voice of Lulu's younger sister:

Why am I alone with you mother?
Where is my sister?
Why is my best sister gone?
And why do you look so angry mother?
I miss my sister I want her back!
Do you miss her as well?
Why is so dark?
I do not want to live without my Lulu.

> Why am I alone whith you mother?
> Where is my sister?
> Why is my best sister gone,
> And why do look Angry Mother?
> I miss my sister I want her back!
> do you miss her aswell?
> why is it so dark? I do not do not
> Want to live with out my Lulu.

Ashley was assessed at low levels of literacy; alarmingly, his writing attainment, as measured by National Curriculum tests, was going backwards.

Ashley	January	July
NC reading	3c	3a
NC writing	2b	2c

He is, however, clearly able to write an interesting, dramatic stanza using as a model the text he has read, enacted and talked about. Taking on a fictional voice, he takes familiar language and gives it a poetic 'spin'. Ashley would not have been able to generate this writing without the substantial preparation provided by Teacher G's extended teaching sequence devoted to the poem (page 34).

Using ICT to enter the world of the poem

Following children's contemporary interpretations of the poem that flowed from extended Book Talk, teachers introduced the interactive software. This was an opportunity for children to re-read the poem on-screen. The software posed questions in order for children to speculate and talk about the puzzles in the story.

Can you find and write down all of the things that were in Lulu's room?

Back to the poem

The software included a (printable) writing prompt (*Dear Mother, I am leaving because...*) and an email address for children to write to Lulu. There was also a link to a CBBC online discussion board about runaways, where children could read what other 8 to 11 year old children had written and post their own thoughts.

Although the research team envisaged children using the software in pairs or small groups around a class computer, it was predominately shown to the whole class in the computer suite with teachers leading the discussions.

With *What Has Happened to Lulu?*, email emerged as significant imaginative writing for boys - even in those classes where children like Omar and Rammone wrote 'pretend' handwritten emails on paper, rather than going online.

However, it was possible for children to email Lulu and get a response. The project researcher opened an email account for the character Lulu (lulu@clpe.co.uk). Boys entered the world of the poem through emails to Lulu, which they wrote individually and collaboratively, asking questions that had been raised in Book Talk discussions. The project researcher would reply in role as Lulu.

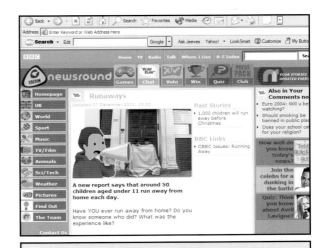

A BBC NEWS REPORT SAYS THAT AROUND 50 CHILDREN AGED UNDER 11 RUN AWAY FROM HOME EACH DAY. CHILDREN HAVE EMAILED THEIR IDEAS AND THOUGHTS ABOUT THE ISSUE TO A CBBC WEBSITE BULLETIN BOARD:

I ran away from home because I had a horrible argument with my Mum and Dad. I was out for a whole night and even though I was close to home, it was still very scary. I felt like I just had to get away at the time, but I wouldn't do it again. I'd stay at a friend's house and at least then there'd be someone to talk to.
    Mandy, 12, Coventry

I ran away from home once, because I thought everyone hated me, I came back after 2 days at a friend's, I realised my family have never hated me and never will!
    Danielle, 10, Chesterfield

I've seen a lot of movies with kids running away from home, and when I was younger I thought it would be quite fun to be a runaway. But, I've wisened up a bit over the past few years. I've learned that running away doesn't help you at all, but makes everything worse.
    Haley, 12, Surrey

Dear Lulu,
Why did you leave in the first place? And why did
you leave your rag doll?If you just wanted to go
away you could just say to your mum I want to be
alone. Where did you go? Was it a safe place to be?
We think that you should pack your bags again and
go back to your mum and talk to her. We think you
were unfair to your mum by just going without
telling her where you were going because she has
raised you and this is the thanks you give her? Take
care of yourself by just telling people where you are
going and they might just let you have a bit of
freedom or what you would like.
Best wishes from Connor and Alfred

Dear Connor and Alfred,
I had to leave my little house - I felt too closed-in
and not free to do what I wanted. I left my rag doll
because I am a big girl now and I am leaving my
toys behind me for good. It's hard to explain - but
I just needed some space to think about what I want
to do. I would like to travel and see the world!
Best wishes from Lulu

Dear Lulu,
Next time could you explain to your Mum why
you should leave because she will be very worried
if you just disappear. Have you tried finding out
your mum's point of view? Lulu, you should
know that it is dangerous to go off at night alone.
Here are some questions for you to answer
because we are puzzled by this poem.

1. Why did you leave?
2. When you left, where did you go?
3. How much money was in the moneybox?
4. When you left did you jump out of the window?
5. Did you take a car with your dad?

6. Why did you leave your shoe behind and why
were you in a rush?
7. When you went why didn't you take your
rag doll?
We hope our questions don't upset you but we
would like to know your point of view.
We hope your problems work out,
best wishes

This form of communication immersed children
in the poem; they would address 'Lulu' directly, without
teacher direction or intervention. As Merchant (2003)
has observed about a separate email project with Year 4
and Year 5 children, these writers are exploring the con-
versational style of electronic communication and in the
process they are creating their own interesting texts.

Independence and self-correction

Ashley and Ali both have difficulties with
transcription; their spelling is poor and their handwriting at the start of the project was virtually illegible. Both
of these factors cause them to write very little. Teacher G
wanted Ashley and Ali to take more responsibility for
their transcription errors, and offered them an
opportunity to email the author of Lulu, the poet
Charles Causley. Using the spellcheck and working
together, they grappled independently with their
spelling difficulties. Their teacher explained to them
how the spellcheck and grammar check worked on their
computer program:

> *Teacher G: "The red line will tell you the spelling is*
> *wrong, what are you going to do? The green line*
> *might tell you that you said something like 'we was*
> *happy' rather than 'we were happy."*

Ashley and Ali wrote:

> *Dear Mr Causley*
> *We have been reading your poems and books at*
> *school. We enjoy them. We espeshaly (corrects to*
> *'especially') lik (corrects to 'like') The Merrymaid*
> *of Zennor because it is a*
>
> *wonderfol*
> *wonderfole*
> *wonderfoal*
> *wonderfoel*
> *wonderfil*
> *wonderfull*
> *wonderful book with real life parts.*

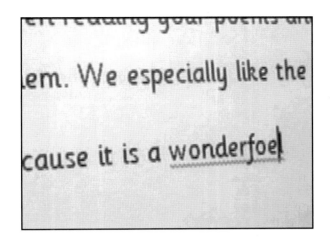

In a discussion afterwards, Teacher G asked the two boys to think about the differences between writing by hand and word processing.

Teacher G: *"What would it have been like if you wrote it by hand?"*

Ali: *"It would have loads of mistakes and be hard to read."*

Teacher G: *"Why do you think you do better on the computer?"*

Ali: *"On the computer you don't have to worry about your handwriting or the spelling because if its spelled wrong or the computer doesn't understand they will put a red line or a green line."*

Teacher G: *"You tried hard spellings - 'especially' and 'wonderful'. What's the difference when you are writing?"*

Ashley: *"When you're writing down, the lines don't come up."*

Teacher G: *"This tells you immediately, doesn't it?"*

Ashley: *"You can be told if you write something wrong."*

Teacher G: *"What I found out Ashley is that you're quite a good speller, but since I can't read your handwriting it's been very hard for me to know what you can and can't spell. Do you think it's still important to have good handwriting?"*

Ali: *"If you are an adult and still can't write properly, you would have to get a computer, but if you don't have enough money you would have to have good handwriting."*

Ashley: *"You can't all your life type on the computer. People will think – this man can't write properly! They'll be laughing at you, when you're an adult."*

Ali: *"If you're writing a script for a film, the person reading it and the person starring in wouldn't know what you said."*

Ashley: *"People who have to read the script won't be able to read it and will make fools out of themselves. It makes you feel big about yourself when you do a whole page of writing."*

Ashley and Ali see a real life purpose for writing and connect the skills they are learning in school to jobs they may one day have as adults. They feel pride in a good piece of writing, and like to be 'told' by the computer when they have made errors. The computer is a type of audience for their writing that can point out their mistakes.

Like Ashley and Ali, other boys in this Years 4 class also emailed the author Charles Causley, via the West Country Writers Association, with questions raised in their Book Talk discussions.

Dear Mr. Causley,
We have been reading your poem What Has
Happened to Lulu? We like this poem because it is a
mystery. When did you write this poem, and how
old is it? Where did you write it? How did you
think of all the ideas? How old is Lulu supposed to
be? Did this happen in real life, and where was it
set? Why does Lulu have a happy rhythm but is a
sad poem? We enjoyed your poem because it rhymes
and it's interesting for us because we like looking for
clues like a detective. It's a great poem but next time
could you draw a picture to illustrate it to make it
more interesting for us and make it more scarier.
We look forward to reading your reply. From
Jamie, Babah, Kenny and Darren

This class received an email reply from a colleague of Charles Causley informing them that he would pass on their communications to the author who was 'not an email man but a snail mail man'. Sadly, they were unable to receive a reply from the author, who died in the Autumn of 2003.

The enthusiasm for emailing led Teacher G to create opportunities for children to email other fictional characters, such as *The Highwayman*, and *Willy the Wimp*. As well as being opportunities for writing creatively, these became opportunities for boys to work independently on spelling, punctuation and sentence construction.

A range of writing around one text

Teacher P used emails to Lulu as a springboard for extended writing, in which children visualised Lulu's room and also wrote to the author of the poem. For boys like Benny in Year 5, a range of writing over days and weeks, in various voices and formats around the same text, was an opportunity to continue to define and expand the narrative, refine his ideas and develop stamina for writing.

Benny's teacher, Teacher P, said frankly that he was a 'very naughty' boy. He was one of those boys who 'never takes [literacy] seriously'. Benny was grouped with Jamel and Kerwin who were labelled the 'trouble boys,' a tag they wore with some pride. They were too cool to appear interested in school literacy. This was a group of 'can-but-don't' boys: they were not practising

and extending their reading and writing skills, and their erratic National Curriculum levels reflected this (see table below). Their scores had no clear pattern - Jamel appeared to make no progress in reading or in writing over two terms in relation to statutory assessment. However, Benny and Kerwin both made visible progress, in Benny's case in both reading and writing:

	January reading, writing		July reading, writing	
Benny	3a	2a	4c	3b
Jamel	3a	3c	3a	3c
Kerwin	3c	3a	3b	4c

In interview, Benny described how he surfed the internet every evening at home, reading a range of entertainment websites and watching cinema trailers. In school writing, he welcomed an opportunity include his own ideas about what could be happening in the poem.

In the following four pieces of writing, Benny responded to the poem in different ways. He wrote in different genres without having to tackle reading a new text at the same time. This approach supported under-achievers such as Benny. Rather than learning a new writing genre (a letter, or a description) through reading a new text or text fragment – an approach that teachers may interpret as implicit in the National Literacy Strategy – each time Benny wrote around *What Has Happened to Lulu?* he had something different to say and new questions to ask, as he built up his ideas about the poem.

Like many children in the project, Benny wanted to write about Lulu in ways that made sense to him. In his writing, he gave Lulu a pair of Barbie shoes and a Nintendo. He suggested that people called her a 'geek' in school because she was neat, tidy and bright. Benny also responded enthusiastically to the opportunity to collaborate with a friend in emailing Lulu in role as one her uncles, and in writing a letter to Charles Causley.

Dear mother, father, and Ken little brother,
I am sorry mother but I have to run away. The way
you treated me was so bad. Tell my little brother that
I am going to miss him. Tell Dad not to drink too
much alcohol. I am going to live at my boyfriend's
house in Scotland. You are free to visit me at 33
Chupny Road. I miss our dog Masy, I hope she misses

*me. I love all of you very much but I am going to live
a better life. Tell my friends at school that I have gone
to live with Uncle Ben and Aunt Mary for a couple
of years. Love from your daughter, Lulu*

*Dear Lulu,
Why was you running away from home? I will advise
you to go home. Your mum is having a bad time, so
are your brother and your sister and dad so please
come back home. I heard that you got to go to
Scotland and you are going to stay there for the rest of
your life. Will you please come home to see your mum
instead of staying over that country for ever? You will
never get a chance to see your mum again, so go back
to England. It is not the same without you. You are so
funny, you make me laugh so much, we miss you so
much. Why did you go away? Where is your money
box and why is there only one shoe on your bed? We
love you,
Your uncles Benny and Jake*

*Lulu's Bedroom
Lulu's room is as fresh as a flowery field. Her money
box is on a black chest. Her bunk bed is yellow and
dark. Her rag doll is a bright blue, a sparkly green
and a hot red. Her shoes are multicoloured. She has
a big pile of homework she has skipped in one of the
many corners of her room. Her fireplace is in the very
corner of her room. All the things in her room are
nice and neat. The floor has not a spot. Lulu is very
neat. People call her geek at school. She lives in a
mansion. She has 17 sheets. The weather outside is so
windy you could see the window going inside and
out. The only thing that was dirty was Lulu's Barbie
shoes. She is very bright. She has 25 books in the
drawer. Her Nintendo is in good condition.*

*Dear Charles Causley,
I liked the poem you did called What Has Happened
to Lulu, very interesting. I liked the rhymes in the
poem but I did not like when the narrator kept on
saying "Mother". I would really like to know where
Lulu is but you did not say it in the poem. I felt very
sorry for Lulu. How did you think about the poem
when you wrote it? Was she a bad teenager? Did she
smoke or do drugs? Was her mother mean or did she
beat her? Was her brother annoying? Yours sincerely,*

Benny's writing reflected his way of speaking *why
was you running away from home?*, and this was a feature
of case study boys' writing overall (see chapter 7). The
poem itself, and certainly the emails, lent themselves
readily to contemporary interpretations and informal
language. However, with teacher intervention and modelling, there were focus boys who were able to write very
differently from the way they talked (see chapter 8).

Evaluations

Children enthusiastically brought their own ideas
and experiences to a discussion of this text, although
these ideas were sometimes challenging for teachers.
Children's interpretations of the poem could be very
different from teachers' interpretations, and this theme
would emerge again when Year 5 classes read and
discussed the Louis Sachar novel.

Children were able to use ICT for discussion and
communications that were simultaneously imaginary
and 'real', through emails to and from Lulu. Teacher G
said: "They can't believe it when I tell them – you've got
mail". Given the long hours of home computer use
reported by boys like Benny, putting the text on screen,
and providing opportunities to email and contribute to
an online discussion board were obvious ways to engage
boys' expertise in and enthusiasm for the computer, in
the interests of their reading and writing in school.

'Drama on paper' allowed boys to write in role as
a mother or as a girl; with preparation, boys were more
than willing take on and write in a female voice.
Enacting the text helped them to develop their ideas and
language and to imagine the world of the text more fully.
Teachers observed that opportunities to dramatise the
text, either through notes and letters in role and emails
to the character, or through performance and
movement, had a positive impact on writing and on
behaviour.

> Teacher P: "*I was astonished that so much work
> could come from one poem. We made a big display
> of the work, but it could have been five or six times
> as big, lots of work in folders, booklets, artwork.*"

> Teacher S: "*I was amazed at the intensity of
> their writing in role, how the drama affected their
> writing.*"

Teacher L: *"I noticed that the boys were very on-task in drama even though they were noisy."*

Teacher K: *"They say 'Oh it's not me writing Miss, it's Lulu' – but of course, it IS them writing."*

Boys in this class commented:
"It's like a mystery"
"It could happen so it's like real life"
"I like being other people"
"I can't believe all this came from one poem"
"It was fun and exciting and we got to talk to each other"

It is doubtful whether *What Has Happened to Lulu?* would be on a list of recommended 'Books for Boys'. On the surface, it has everything working against it: it's a poem, it's about a girl, the language and the setting are old-fashioned. Yet boys' comments, discussion, enactment, writing and behaviour for learning in this chapter tell a different story: literacy was 'fun' and 'exciting', it was 'like real life', and boys wanted to be a part of it.

The Seal Wife

Experiences before, during and after writing:

The traditional short story *The Seal Wife* is a British fairy tale originating from the Scottish islands. There are several versions of this story and Kevin Crossley-Holland has included it in his anthologies of folk tales from the British Isles (2001). He describes it as one of many 'selkie' stories which link the lives of human beings and seals. In the story, a fisherman sees a seal shed its coat and turn into a beautiful woman. He falls in love with her and steals her seal skin so she will live on the land with him. She begs him to return her seal coat, but instead he hides it from her. Years pass and they have children. One day, the children discover the hidden seal coat. The seal wife takes it, tells her children she is leaving them 'for a little while' and returns to her home in the ocean. As she leaves she tells the fisherman, "I loved you, but I have always loved my seal husband more."

Like the Charles Causley poem, and unexpectedly for some of the project teachers, this short story again provoked animated discussion amongst children – about

the moral issue of stealing another man's wife and imprisoning her, the real meaning of 'love', and having to choose between your children and your 'true' life. There was also intense speculation about the fate of the children the seal wife left behind – would they grow webbed feet? Would they ever see their mother again? From these discussions, classes wrote their own versions of the story as retellings, continuations, or from a particular character's point of view.

Teachers used CLPE software which was developed to go with this text. The software presentation briefly recounts the story, asks questions about the characters' dilemmas and provides links to websites of online readings of other Selkie and mermaid stories. Some teachers felt that the online reading was too difficult for their classes, and some teachers were also reluctant to allow children onto the internet unsupervised. Like the 'Lulu' software, this programme was intended for pairs or small groups of children to use independently to extend their understanding of the text. However, in most cases it was the teacher who led these discussions, either in the classroom or in the computer suite.

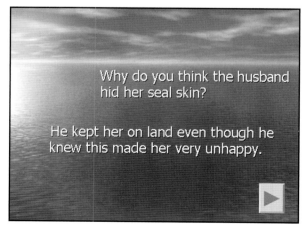

There were differences in the quality of talk that took place in the six classrooms. A concern sometimes voiced by teachers was that children did not have sufficient experience to discuss their reading in a meaningful way, and that without teacher intervention children's discussions would sometimes flounder. However, in classrooms where teachers themselves were strong models of purposeful talk, talk between children reached a higher level.

After reading - before writing

Talk: 'There is the dilemma'

Two teachers (Teachers S & K) provided children with written talk prompts to make sure they 'stayed on track' in their group discussions about the story - for example:

1) *How do you think the man felt when he saw the seal woman for the first time?*
2) *What do you think was going through the man's head when he decided to steal her skin?*
3) *Do you think the man acted in the correct way when the woman pleaded with him to have her skin back?*
4) *How do you think the seal woman felt when she said she would marry him?*
5) *After some time of living with the man and his children how do you think the seal woman felt?*
6) *Why do you think the man acted how he did? Was he right to act in that way?*

Teacher K directed her Year 5 class, as homework, to tell the story to some one at home before discussing the story in class. Kenneth and Yusuf, a Caribbean Heritage and a Somali boy in this class, both have some difficulties writing and spelling standard English. Their telling the story to siblings at home was the beginning of their internalizing the story and its literary language. Using talk prompts, they discussed the story on their 'Talk Table' during the Literacy Hour, with Rammone and Danny:

Yusuf: "*I told the story to my little sister and she felt sad and confused because the mother leaves her children. But it's right, because he stole another man's wife.*"

Kenneth: "*My brother said it was weird and freaky, when she takes the skin off and puts it on*

again. How did she do that? Wouldn't she die or something?"

Yusuf: "*She left him, but he deserved it because he stole another man's love.*"

Kenneth: "*It was love at first sight, but it was all in his head. He blackmails her.*"

Danny: "*It's his only chance to get some one. She's special. And she did love him, she said - "I have always loved you."*"

Rammone: "*I give it a 10.*"

Their exchanges reflected their understandings of, and questions about, the fictional events. They talked about the story in informal contemporary language: *weird, freaky, it was all in his head.*

Although written prompts did keep discussions focused, children sometimes seemed more concerned with having a correct answer to the written question than with discussing the question. Some children even felt compelled to write answers to the talk prompts, even though teachers would clearly say that "you do not need to write anything down."

Open-ended questioning seemed to elicit wider-ranging responses in which children would often call upon their personal experiences. In Teacher G's class, Okieriete immediately referred the story of the mother who tells her children she is leaving them 'for a little while' to his own life:

"*My mum went to Ghana for a long time, and even though she was gone she called me on the telephone all the time so I knew she always still loved me.*"

In Teacher S's class, children also related the Selkie story to other, familiar narratives:

Leon: "*It reminds me of the movie "Splash" when they're in the restaurant and some water gets on her and her mermaid body starts to grow.*"

Research officer: "*This story makes me so sad! Why would some one write such a sad story?*"

Jermaine: "*Maybe it happened for real to someone that their mother left them, and they wanted to let people know how it feels.*"

Omar: *"You can't force some one to live with you. You can't decide other people's lives. If I was the children I would feel sad, I would grow up and never know what my mother looked like, even her grandchildren would never know their grandmother."*

Jermaine: *"She should have explained to the children what she was going to do."*

Omar: *"I could write: The seal wife – part two! She comes back – or he goes into the ocean with the children and she brings them all seal skins."*

Jermaine said the discussion was a good way to get ideas which he would use later in writing his own story of the seal wife:

"This is OK, to work with a partner, because then I get to understand their ideas as well as mine, so I can get a mixture of both ideas, instead of just having mine... I found it a bit helpful because I get to know how I would put my characters and how they would feel, I can put like expressions of how they would feel instead of making it a boring story...It helps me think about how life would be, with people like this, how they would go and steal people, and pretend it's their family but I don't

think it's right. Shouldn't it really hurt inside, to know it wasn't really yours, that they were just captured? He's all happy but she and her family is not. Instead of making both lives happy, he's ruined one and made his happy."

Teacher P's discussion with a group of children (two boys and a girl) shows a teacher in a real conversation with pupils; this is, as Chambers (1993) describes, an adult who is helping children to enjoy reading. At the same time, Teacher P is modelling 'book talk' and extending the children's language and ideas about the text. This discussion took place around a laptop computer, with Teacher P and the children using the CLPE software to recall, and then talk about, the story:

Teacher P: *Perhaps we can jot down some ideas on paper. Why did he steal her seal skin?*

A: *Because he loved her too much.*

Teacher P: *Very well put, he didn't just love her SO much, he actually loved her TOO much for everyone's good.*

A: *He's thinking he should let her go, but he just can't do it.*

Teacher P: *How can you make some one very unhappy because you love them? There is the dilemma.*

A: *If he loved her he should let her make her own choices, he could let her go back for a little while.*

Teacher P: *Was it a lie? Did she know she was never coming back?*

A: *Even if it was a lie, she knows she couldn't tell the truth because it would upset the children.*

N: *She comes back in spirit*

T: *Old memories come back to her, she thinks about them. The children remember her and how she used to be.*

Teacher P: *Why does he say 'it was my fault'?*

T: *It was the depression what she had, because he had her sealskin. It was his fault because he hurt her. He must have loved her THAT much if he would never let her go. If he did let her go, she might not come back. if you truly love some one, you will do anything to make them happy.*

Teacher P: *Including giving them freedom. Because it's not just a case of you loving them –*

A: *They have to love you, too. She's waited such a long time for freedom. She might not want to come back. He regrets it.*

T: *I would feel devastated if I was one of the children. To find out that your dad is trapping your mum.*

A: *I would be experiencing the leaving.*

Teacher P: *Yes you would be suffering that loss yourself.*

A: *I would feel worse and worse. It's better to have both your parents*

N: *The children might not want her to come back, she might lie again. They don't trust her.*

A: *He might steal her skin again and the children wouldn't tell her this time where it is. She might hide it herself, so she could find it herself. It's her cherished possession.*

Teacher P: *That might be a solution.*

A: *If he changed, he would put the skin where she could find it.*
Teacher P: *Will she take that risk?*

A: *One chance in a million. It is worth trying. There might be a big reward. You might have your family AND your freedom.*

This interaction is an example of how 'guided reading' can be an extended talk about the text. It is a real *discussion* about reading in which the teacher is genuinely interested in the children's ideas. They in turn are not answering 'right/wrong' questions that test their comprehension of the text in a limited way, but are engaging with the dilemma of the story, and the conflicting feelings of the characters. They are also imagining different outcomes or endings to the story.

Visualisation: I could see the cliffs...

Teacher L directed children to use 'overnight thinking time' before discussing and writing about the story:

"I really thought it wouldn't work, that no one would remember to do it – but they came in the next day and they all had a lot more to say about it, some really good ideas, because they had talked to some one at home about it."

In a whole-class discussion, children visualized a climactic moment in the story in which the seal wife returns to her home in the ocean. Teacher L scribed some of the language generated by this shared visualization onto a white board.   Children then wrote this moment of the story independently:

The wind was howling as I shouted "MOTHER! MOTHER!" But the wind took my breath away. She was just about to dive into the sea when a thunderbolt hit the shore. Then she saw me and gave me a blowing-kiss as she dived into the sea. I felt flabbergasted. I felt terrible and I never saw her again. (Murad)

I was with my mum on the rocks one stormy night. I was nine years old. I knew there was something different about her. She said goodbye to me. I begged her not to jump but the wind snatched my voice. I ran up to her. "Please don't jump" I pleaded. But she dived in. "No No No Noo!" I dropped on the sand, my shoulders in my hands. A hand touched me. It was my Dad. "She would never ever forget about you Mike." (Bairoh)

I could see the cliffs. My beloved wife was standing on the rocks waiting to go in the deep dark sea. As the water touched her leg it reminded me of the words of truth. And there she stood like the Statue of Liberty. (Alhassan)

Murad, Bairoh and Alhassan used their experiences in oral rehearsal to create dynamic, intense scenes in a few lines of writing. An opportunity to visualise, to have a picture in their minds, created a springboard for writing in the voice of the seal wife's abandoned child or husband. The writers take on first-person voices of fictional characters and also their physical, literal point of view; we as readers 'see' what the characters are seeing. Bearne (2002: 67) notes that because of widespread access to multimedia and multimodal texts, "...young writers now draw on highly visual material for their sources and inspiration." It was striking that Alhassan, born and raised in South London, called on an image of the Statue of Liberty to describe the seal wife returning to the sea.

This writing was a 'caption' to the children's visualised pictures rather than a narrative. Although these paragraphs were powerful, they were not extended into longer pieces of writing. Because increasing the quantity as well as the quality of boys' writing was an urgent matter for teachers, we wanted to look in some detail at where and how children developed and wrote whole texts.

A teaching sequence

In the first step of an extended teaching sequence (page 34) Teacher S, after telling the story to her class, also asked children to visualise or 'see' the ocean and the seals in the story, and then to write these visualisations into one paragraph. Kwaku, whose first language is Twi, wrote about the picture in his mind; like Alhassan, he can 'see' the story:

> *I can see in my picture a glamorous blue and green sparkling sea and a sandy beach with seaweed strewn along the beach. I can see a brown wooden little house with an open fire outside the house. I can see smooth grey seals jumping in and out of the sea, making noises in the sea. (Kwaku)*

Using paint and pastels, the class transferred these visualisations in words to images in artwork. Throughout this teaching sequence, Teacher S would create opportunities for children to sketch or draw as they wrote their stories, often to their disbelief: "They couldn't believe it when I said they could leave spaces for drawings in their first draft."

From mind-map to story

After painting and drawing their visualisations, children created mind-maps of the story's different locations: the sea, the fisherman's cottage, the beach. They wrote words or phrases linked to these locations, as a rough writing plan. Unlike a writing frame or formal plan that depicts a sequential beginning, middle and end, these mind-maps were non-linear. They were pictorial ways of seeing the world of the story as a whole and depicting that world in outline. Mind-maps showed the 'shape' of the story-world, rather than a sequence of events. Focus boys in the project used this type of planning effectively, learning to expand the writing about the setting and around the action, rather than driving the narrative action forward.

Both Jermaine and Kwaku started the project with low levels of assessed literacy as measured by National Curriculum tests. Jermaine in particular was a boy that puzzled Teacher S, who said that he "just never seems to understand what he's doing, he's always so confused." Jermaine produced a lot of writing, but he found it difficult to sustain and control his ideas. For him, the new type of story plan was revelatory:

> *"Instead of just writing it and you don't know how to set the scene, you do this and it helps you plan out what the houses would look like and what the beach would look like and what the sea would look like. It helps you instead of having to write it and write it – standing there waiting and thinking for the ideas, you waste all your time just thinking. It helps me*

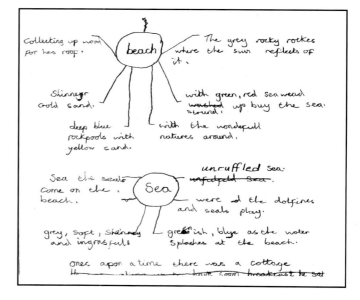

knowing what I'm about to write. Instead of sitting there and not knowing what I'm about to write, then I can just get on with it and have it done, as quickly as I can. It saves me sitting here, and it makes me work more, because I've got my ideas in my head, and it helps me."

Jermaine's impassioned description of the pains and problems of planning is a reminder that conventional planning does not always help young writers. For him, preparation for writing is far more helpful than planning for writing. What matters most to him is that he should be able to 'see' the situation, and 'get his ideas in his head,' which he has been able to do through discussion and visualisation.

From the mind maps and initial visualisation, children began to write their stories. Here is Kwaku's first chapter:

A long time ago, when the world was young, lived a fisherman called Kane. Kane lived in a little wooden cottage. He lived near a rocky beach. He fished for a living. Every day he went fishing on the beach. It was very quiet on the beach when he was fishing, but one day it wasn't. Once on a rainy day he was walking on the beach feeling unhappy and miserable. All of a sudden he heard a strange noise. He heard it again. Then the noise stopped for a little while. He hid behind a large rock and peered over to see what the noise was. Kane was watching the seals and strangely these three beautiful seals cheered him up. Strangely he saw the three seals taking off their seal coats. Kane saw three beautiful women dancing and singing. One of them caught his eye so he decided to take the seal coat so she could live with him.

Here Kwaku's writing shows that he is hearing and seeing this scene from the viewpoint of the fisherman. He emphasises the fisherman's mood and the 'strange' change in this mood as he watches the apparition and transformation of the seal-women. Kwaku does not skip anything, he builds up the beginning of the story slowly and well, leading up to Kane's spur of the moment decision to steal the seal coat belonging to one of the women. He is able to do so because he has thoroughly imagined and internalised the story through visualisation, discussion and mind-mapping.

During writing

Teacher S reminded writers of their overarching role in relation to the story: "You are the omnipresent narrator – you know what's going to happen in your story, but the reader doesn't." After a first draft of story-writing, children in S's class exchanged their drafts with an editing partner and read each other's writing using a series of prompts for that specific text:

1) *Have they described where the story is set?*
2) *Have they introduced the fisherman and given some information about his character?*
3) *Have they described the beach and the day when the strange events took place?*
4) *Have they described how the fisherman felt when he saw the seals take off their coats and begin to dance?*
5) *Have they described the dancing ladies?*
6) *Have they described how upset the woman felt when she had to leave the sea?*
7) *Are they writing using sentences?*
8) *Write two positive comments about their work.*

These notes for partner-editing again helped children to see that certain things must not be left out if their stories were to make sense to a reader. The prompts encouraged children to do more thinking about the story-world and the characters, rather than offering a 'story-ladder' emphasis on beginning, middle and end. Children relished the chance to 'mark' their classmate's writing in the role of the teacher, and they took their editing responsibilities seriously.

This class again discussed the story in groups. In the computer suite, they used the CLPE software for further discussion and reading. These opportunities for group and whole class discussion enabled children to add ideas to their stories, identify any gaps in their texts and to finalise their drafts. They illustrated their final copies and returned to the computer suite to download images to create book jackets, including blurbs and excerpts from imaginary reviews.

To complete the writing experience, Jermaine and others from his Year 5 class read their seal stories to children in Reception and Year One classes during Book Week.

How will you deal with the dilemma of choosing between your family and the pull of the sea?

"This amazing magical story tells you how people can be selfish and how they can love"

THE GUARDIAN

RUN AWAY SEAL

Jermaine wrote a Seal Woman chapter book with detailed illustrations. In it, he has reflected all of the multifaceted preparation he has had for his writing: visualization, mind-mapping, discussion, drawing, re-drafting and thinking:

The Seal Woman

Once upon a time there was a cottage. The cottage was made of old shipwrecked wood. It had a display of beautiful white shells above the old fashioned cooker. It had old wooden windows with frosty ice on them. Living in the house was a fisherman called Jack. He was very lonely as he lived by himself.

He got up and turned around to grab his brown, fat and woolly coat. As he walked up to it the old wooden floor boards creaked. He opened the door and a gust of ice cold, frosty and chilly breeze shot up his spine. He forced his way outside and slammed the door behind him. It was like a snow storm scattering all over the place as it clashed along

his body. He could almost see the grey rocks covered with snow. All around him was white as if he was in the sea. Jack bent down and picked up the broken pieces of wood and dusted off the snow. The sea was clashing against the frozen ice as the rapids bashed along the beach. Then he decided to come back in before he was blown away. He struggled to the door. He managed to slide in and with all his might he closed the door. As he was about to sit down the kettle boiled. He took off his old woolly coat and drank his hot, steamy and boiling cocoa. He threw himself on the old soft bed and went to sleep.

One day he woke up and went outside. It was sunny and he saw that the sea was unruffled and the sun was shining and the sea washed up green seaweed. The rock pools had little fishes and lobsters. The crabs scattered all over the place boring themselves underground. Then as the grey clouds started to scatter it started to rain heavily, and he decided to shelter under a big grey rock.

Once upon a time there was a cottage the cottage was made of old ship wreck wood. It had a display of beautiful white shells above the old fashion cooker. It had old wooden windows with frosty ice on them. Living in the houes was a fisher man called Jack was very lonely as he lived by his slef. He got up and turned around to grab his brow, fat and wooly coat as he walked up to it the old wooden floor boards creak. He opened the door and a gust of ice cold, frosty and chilly breeze shot up his spine. He force his way out side and slammed the door behind him it was like a snow scrom scattering all over the place as it clashed along his body. He could allmost see the grey rocks covered with snow all around him was white as if he was in the sea. Jack bent down and picked up the broken pieces of wood and dust off the snow. The sea was clashing against the frozen ice as the rappeds bashed along the beach. Then he dicided to come back in before he was blown away he scruggled to the door. He mange to slide in and with all his might he

He closed the door. As he was about to sit down the kettle boiled he took of his old wooly coat and drankt his hot, steamy and boiling cocoa. He throw his slef on the old soft, bed and went to sleep. One day he woke up and went out side it was sunny and he saw that the sea was unruffled and the sun was shining and the sea whashed up green sea weed. The rock poles had little fishes and lobsters the crabs scatterd all over the place bering there slef under ground. Then as the grey clouds started to oatthered it started to rain heavenly then he dicied to shelter under a big grey rock.

The Attack

Then in the misty fog was a glimmering light that damage his eyes he peered his head around and saw three beautiful laddies. In amazement he crawl up to them silently. The laddies was wearing long dress made of silk and had leather gloves. There voice sound like starts singing in mide moonlight. But one of them suddley couth his eye he thought it was a dream at priss But it wasn't. He went closer then "Snap"!!! he grab the coat and ran of while the other laddies scattered back into the deep blue sea. The waves started clashing, bashing and roaring as the fisher man ran home.

Running to him pleading was the lady who he stolen the coat from. As the man reached the door he ran up to the barn and quickly trampled throw the straw and hid the coat

In a old weby place in the rathers of the barn. "Bang" "Bang"!!! went the door the fisherman came running down the rathers "clatter" "clatter" as the feet banged on the floor. He opened the door and the gril stared the begag for her coat back he. Said "come and live with me" the ladies had no choice becaues she had no where to go. Two mouths past and they got married. Three years later they had three children druing there years the man was very kind and jenros to her but touley she really wanted to go back to the sea where she can be free.

The Attack

Then in the misty fog was a glimmering light that damaged his eyes. He peered his head around and saw three beautiful ladies. In amazement he crawled up to them silently. The ladies were wearing long dresses made of silk and had leather gloves. Their voices sounded like singing in the moonlight. But one of them suddenly caught his eye.
He thought it was a dream at first but it wasn't. He went closer then "Snap!" he grabbed the coat and ran off while the other ladies scattered back into the deep blue sea. The waves started clashing, bashing and roaring as the fisherman ran home.

Running to him, pleading, was the lady who he had stolen the coat from. As the man reached the door he ran to the barn and quickly trampled through the straw and hid the coat in an old webby place in the rafters of the barn. "Bang Bang!" went the door. The fisherman came running down the rafters, "clatter clatter" as his feet banged on the floor. He opened the door and the girl started begging for her coat back. He said, "Come and live with me". The lady had no choice because she had no where to go. Two months passed and they got married. Three years later they had three children. During these years the man was very kind and generous to her, but truly she really wanted to go back to the sea where she can be free.

The Runaway Seal

One day the children were playing and they kept on seeing their dad hide this most glamorous thing in the straw stack. One day the children decided to go and investigate what was in the corn stack, so they went in the barn and pulled out a silver, sparkling and grey coat. They all stood shocked around the most glamorous thing. One night when their mum was tucking them in bed they said, "Mum, mum, dad has hidden a coat in the corn stack" whispered the children.

"Oh has he" said the mother crossly. The next morning they woke up to expect a nice breakfast but she wasn't there. The place was not clean or tidy. They ran up to their dad's bedroom. "Dad, dad, mum is gone!" cried the children.

"What, what you must be joking" yawned dad. The dad got up and went down the stairs tripping up on the way. They searched and searched, trashing the place, the kitchen, bathroom and the bedroom. The dad shouted "Stop!" Everyone froze. "Come here" he said "I got to tell you something". They sat down and dad told them the story about their mum. Every day they would walk alone on the beach with their hearts sank. They wondered what seal is their mum.

One day the dad was going to the beach to fish. When he walked out he saw three big, fat and juicy fish. His mouth grew wide in amazement. He looked up and saw a glimpse of a fat thing slide back into the sparkling water. Then the fisherman knew that he was not alone.

Jermaine used his mind map to develop each scene fully: the cottage, the seashore and the 'attack' on the sand. During the writing of his first draft, he was observed to refer to his mind map regularly, turning back the pages of his writing book to check words and phrases he had mapped around each scene. In his final copy, he punctuated each chapter and narrative transition with an illustration. Using these visual elements in planning and in drafting helped him to control the pace and content of his writing.

As if to confirm this, in an interview, Jermaine said he was pleased with how he wove together drawing and writing in his story:

I writed it till I was about there (points to first section of writing), *then I decided to do a picture there, then I write again. I drawed it first. …It reminds me of things that I watched that are exciting. I like the drawings that I done in it as well. And the descriptions. … It reminded me of things that I'd seen and it helped me do my drawings. It really helps in stories watching TV and films to help your stories and get ideas from them, and make stories out of it.*

Jermaine's story is a fully-imagined world. In the long descriptive first section, Jermaine takes a detailed look around this world and evokes the fisherman's hard daily life before ever the action starts. He has, in his teacher's words, become the 'omnipresent narrator'. As the writer, he understands that readers will not know what is coming next in his story, and so he leaves nothing out. In his writing, he creates a story full of sounds, images and movement. In spite of this, Jermaine confessed that he was still not confident about story-writing:

"I find it very hard to write stories. Sometimes you're blank of ideas and you need ideas so you have to go somewhere to get the ideas, but where you go, they've already written it, or it's not already written but it's too hard to put in the story, so you got to think of a way and it seems to you like impossible, you can't think of a way. That's what makes it so hard to write stories."

Yet it was apparent that Jermaine – with the experiences and preparation of this two-week teaching sequence around the story - was capable of writing a sophisticated story that deployed powerful shifts of mood. It was interesting to hear him describe writing in a visual way, about being 'blank' of ideas as if his mind were a canvas on which he projected the 'things' that he's seen on TV and in films.

A significant breakthrough for Jermaine was that his writing was very different from the way he normally spoke. His writing is not like his speech written down, he took on the the rhythms of Kevin Crossley-Holland's retelling. He was composing with, and controlling, written language forms. By the end of the two terms of the project, although there was no change in Jermaine's National Curriculum reading level, both he and Kwaku had made clear progress in writing.

NC Levels	January Reading	January Writing	July Reading	July Writing
Jermaine	2a	2b	2a	3b
Kwaku	2b	2b	3c	3b

Group work: telling, re-telling and collaborative writing

Teachers asked children to re-tell the story, in order to develop their experience of narrative through oral story-telling. Teacher G's Year 4 class would tell the story going around in a circle, with each child who

spoke holding a 'magic stone' or 'hagstone' which was then passed on to the next speaker. Teacher G reported that this exercise in continuing a narrative was initially difficult for many children: "They found it really hard remembering what would come next" and, as a form of enactment, she encouraged them to incorporate gestures as they spoke – for example, wringing their hands in the 'pleading' scene where the seal woman begs for the return of her skin. From these retellings, children in Teacher G's class in pairs wrote the 'pleading' scene as a dialogue:

(Priscilla as the Seal woman) (pleading); *Please! Please! Give me back my seal fur. I will die without it. I've got children. They need food.*

(Wilfred as MacCodrum): I WILL GIVE IT BACK BUT YOU HAVE TO MARRY ME. I'M BESOTTED ALL BECAUSE OF YOU.

Seal Woman: *But! But! I can't marry you. I have got a husband all ready.*

MacCodrum: I DON'T CARE. I JUST WANT YOU TO MARRY ME.

Seal Woman (crossly): *What do you mean you don't care? He will die a broken man without me.*

MacCodrum: SO WHAT DIE A BROKEN MAN. YOU'RE JOKING, WHEN MY WIFE DIED I DID NOT DIE A BROKEN MAN.

Seal Woman (not sure): *OK I will marry you.*

MacCodrum (happily): THE WEDDING IS TOMORROW.

These shared compositions were extended into longer pieces of collaborative writing, in which groups of children continued the story of the seal children and what became of them. Children working together extended the narrative, added thoughts and dialogue, and changed episodes to create longer, more complex stories. These stories which we discuss in chapter 7 were initially drafted on large paper so that changes and additions could easily be inserted and read.

Entering the world of the story through performance and drama

The children in Teacher G's class wanted to perform and videotape their stories. Before the performances, children spontaneously brought to school a range of props scavenged from home: a fisherman's cap, plastic fish for the 'ocean', a furry vest for a seal coat, and a long black wig for the seal wife to wear. As one child read out the text, other members of the writing group would mime and act it out, and would echo dialogue read by the narrator. From oral story-telling and mime, children went on to enact their own writing (see chapter 7).

In another successful drama session following the reading of the story, Teacher P became the Judge presiding over arguments in 'The Seal Wife in Divorce Court.' The written arguments for the prosecution and the defence were drafted collaboratively, with groups contributing ideas for what each character would say in defence of his or her actions. The collaborative drafts were subsequently refined in individual writing and read out in performative readings, with the classroom tables

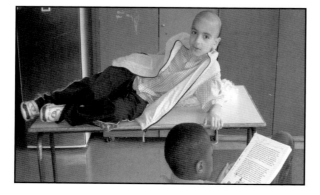

and chairs re-arranged as a courtroom. In this sequence, two of the 'trouble boys,' Kerwin and Jamel, make their cases eloquently:

Teacher P as the Judge: *The court is in session, and I will remind everyone that no one may speak without addressing me first. This court is convened to hear arguments about whether MacCodrum the fisherman is right to demand the return of his wife, the Seal Woman, to whom he is legally still married since in the eyes of the law they have not been divorced. And in fact we will hear first from the Seal Wife who has traveled at some considerable distance from the ocean and appears in great distress, you may speak:*

Melvin as the Seal Woman: *My name is the Seal Woman and I am 35 years old. I have a right to take all of my belongings without sharing with MacCodrum. MacCodrum had no right at all stealing my skin and my freedom. I realize that the children don't deserve to grow up without me because it will devastate them. It was wrong to steal someone's freedom like MacCodrum did to me and ruin my life by holding me and imprisoning me by taking my skin. I love him deep deep down but I hate the fact that he stole my skin and for interfering in my life. I can't forgive MacCodrum for stealing my skin and my freedom which was wrong. My life belongs to the sea with all of my children together. But if I leave MacCodrum I will break his heart and he might die of loneliness or could commit crimes.*

Teacher P: *Thank you, your statement is very persuasive. However, we will now hear from one of your children on the land who, as I understand it, feels he has been abandoned by you, his mother – are you prepared to speak now?*

Kerwin as a land child: *If you go Mummy I don't get good food, Dad can't cook.*
I don't get new shoes, Dad is lazy.
I don't get medicines Mummy, Dad spends the money.
If you go Mummy who will help us with our homework?
Who will discipline us? Who will read us bed time stories?
If you go Mummy who will look after us, Dad is too drunk.
Who will take us to school while Dad is partying?

Please please don't go Mummy, stay with us, if you go our life will be miserable.
Father will be a stupid, drunk and broken hearted man.

Teacher P: *Thank you for your statement, which I will take into consideration. Certainly your situation is very serious and the interests of children are paramount in this case. You may sit down. I now call upon one of the seal children who is here with his father, the seal husband.*

Jamel as a seal child: *We are the seal children. We were very angry, sad and disappointed because our mother left us for five years. We the sea children had difficulty at sea school because when we had home-work we had no one to help us. When our mother came to visit us, we didn't know who she was and she was shocked that we didn't know her. One of us thought that we had just a father and not a mother. When she came back we children were almost fully grown seals. My brother's age was 9 years old and I was 10 years old. We love our mum on one side and on the other side we were disappointed with her because she left us for five years.*

Teacher P created a very strong 'frame' for this drama. It worked differently from hot-seating or thought-tracking, in which one or two children speak in role while others ask questions. In 'Divorce Court', children's independent writing took place in the context of other writing and in the framework of a larger, over-arching text.

Teacher P was firm about the ground rules for this drama activity: "They wanted at first to make it like Jerry Springer! I couldn't really allow that. So we had to have a long discussion about the rules of the courtroom."

The solemnity of this situation, and the formal style set by the judge, gave this writing a special resonance and made children draw on their powers of persuasion and argument. All of the children took part and each one played a part in this drama. Melvin, Kerwin and Jamel's individual texts are interesting, but read together they acquire deeper meaning and power, and create a larger, even more coherent text.

Evaluations

Teaching that planned for experiences before, during, and after writing had a positive impact on underachievers who needed time to grasp the narrative and language of a story and make these meaningful to themselves as readers and as writers. With these experiences, children continued to develop the control necessary for extended writing. It should be pointed out that this extended teaching time around a text was also

beneficial to high achievers, who were able to write at much more length than they would in a faster-paced literacy curriculum.

In the most successful discussions, talk was open-ended and teachers themselves were strong models of language, demonstrating how talk should take place and go forward. Children were able to bring their own ideas to discussions and integrate these with new language and concepts from the text.

Talk was integrated into the writing process as a time to reflect on what had already been written and to gather ideas to move forward. 'Overnight thinking time', retelling a story at home, group discussions and the use of editing partners were all effective in encouraging children to think and talk about their reading and writing inside and outside of the classroom.

'Seeing' the big shape of the story, in mind-mapping and visualisations, gave children non-linear frameworks from which to begin writing. Physically and orally entering the world of the story, through re-telling and enactment, also helped children experience the over-arching structure of the text.

Opportunities to collaborate and perform their writing encouraged children to work together to create high-quality texts. Weaker writers could also participate in these joint productions, adding their ideas and experiencing the narrative as a whole without having to write it all themselves. Bringing individual pieces of writing together, as part of a whole class drama, helped underachievers make sense of the whole text as they played their parts in it.

Actual or virtual audiences, addressed through performances, through readings and through web publishing, inspired whole classes to write. Both writing and artwork were published on the project website, where teachers and children could read and compare different writing around the same text. Parents were also able to see class work and to leave messages on the website's guestbook. Nothing motivated children more than to know that their work would be published on the world wide web.

There's a Boy in the Girls' Bathroom

Taking risks with texts

The novel by Louis Sachar was chosen for its contemporary appeal. Sachar's work strikes a chord with older children. His books are fun, but they also have a moral dimension that engages readers and involves them in thinking about the characters' problems and dilemmas. There's a Boy in the Girls' Bathroom is about a 'bad' boy who is always in trouble at school but who is sensitive inside and talks to his soft toys at home. In the course of the novel he establishes a relationship with the school learning mentor, makes new friends, and starts to change. At the time of the project, many children were familiar with Sachar as the author of the novel *Holes* which had just become a movie; many children had already seen trailers online.

Choice and control over reading

The research team was interested in how far boys exercised choice and control over their reading in school, and how and when they might choose to socialise or network around reading. Following the classroom-based research of Gemma Moss (1999), which observed girls readily networking around texts in a way that boys did not, teachers picked up Moss's suggestions about the need to consciously encourage networking among boys. They also aimed to see whether boys would voluntarily write at more length in school about texts that personally interested them.

Before the introduction of the novel, the research team looked at boys' reading records over the two terms of the project, as an indicator of what and how much they were reading, and how their reading might be linked to literacy teaching. In the participating classrooms reading records included teachers' notes from guided reading sessions, parents' comments in PACT folders and children's own lists of books read.

Boys in four of the five schools took reading books home on a regular basis, whilst one school was in the process of rethinking its home-school reading scheme. Of the case study pool of boys, 20 out of 24 boys took reading books home in PACT folders between one and three times a week. Boys chose these books themselves and reported reading them once or twice a day, typically "about 20 minutes at a time," or "before bed."

In year 5, boys like Jermaine were taking home longer reading books, sometimes for weeks at a time:

March	*The Unsinkable Titanic*
April	*The Stranger from Somewhere*
May	*Diggory and the Boa Constrictor*
June	*Grace the Pirate*
	Perseus and the Gorgon Medusa
	The Twelve Labours of Heracles

Boys like Ashley in Teacher G's Year 4 class were taking home a wide range of picture books and changing them often:

March	*What's the Time?*
	Baily the Big Bully
	The Hare and the Tortoise
	Dear Greenpeace
	Over in the Meadow
April	*Daniel and the Lions*
	King of the Woods
	Only a Cat
May	*Scrumpy*
	Mouse Soup
	The Party in the Sky
	The Hairy Toe
	To Neal
	Gallo and Xorro
	Bimwili and Zimwili

Reading diaries offered spaces where boys could write freely about their choices in reading, and sometimes their mothers might also write a comment:

"I hate the Zimwili because he made Bimwili sing in the drum for his personal pleasure and made her sing. But when it got to her home village to play, everybody think that when he hit the drum it sings, the drum sings but the family freed her. That's real good." (Ashley)

"Jermaine read well, he started at pg 24 and became more fluent by pg 30. He seemed to make more mistakes when he was rushing, eg fell = flew. He finished pg 34 with just that mistake. Damn good effort son!" (Jermaine's mother)

In school, boys read individually to Learning Support Assistants, and during quiet reading times, usually after lunch or towards the end of the day. Teachers selected books for guided reading based on an assessment of a group's reading ability, and the reading of these texts was sometimes reinforced by word and sentence level work.

The reading books which boys took home included those books that many of them enjoyed reading, such as Jacqueline Wilson and Darren Shan novels, *Lord of the Rings* and the Harry Potter series. Overall, however, a very narrow range of school literacy work emanated from boys' personal reading choices. They wrote about their reading in the form of comments in their reading diaries and, occasionally, in the form of book reports.

The reading environment in most classes was limited. One Year 4 class had a dedicated, colourful, comfortable and child-friendly book area with a wide range of fiction and non-fiction texts including picture books for older readers. Teacher K's Year 5 class shared such an area with a parallel class, but this space was also used regularly for artwork and other non-reading activities. Small classrooms, lack of space and shared resources often limited what teachers felt they were able to offer in terms of a reading environment.

Reading Circles

Danny in Teacher K's Year 5 class, is a 'can and do' reader. He was the only one of the 24 boys identified by teachers who expressed strong preferences and tastes in authors. He has read the Narnia books and his favourite author in the Spring term was Darren Shan. At home he reads Darren Shan's and other authors' websites and also reads and plays on websites such as BBC *Revisewise* and CBBC. Writing, however, seems to be a line he will not cross. He writes just enough to satisfy the teacher's requirements. Although Danny's writing throughout the project continued to be minimal, his teacher did succeed in involving him in motivating some of his peers.

Danny has high status in the class as an able reader. He sets the pace and style - whatever he is reading, all the other boys want to read – or at least *be seen* to be reading. Teacher K organized a twice-weekly session outside of the class in which Danny could choose a book and read to his friends. Two other boys in the group (Rammone and Alfie) were 'can't and don't readers' who often avoided the teacher's attempts to engage them in reading; in Year 5 they were reading phonetically, such as "ed-ghe" for "edge". At the time of observation, this group was reading one of the Narnia Chronicles and only Danny was able to read it fluently and with full understanding. The trio took it in turns to read, with Danny sometimes reading word-for-word along with the less able readers.

This collaboration and peer support seemed to combine a number of benefits. Because they were reading with a high-status boy, underachievers were willing to tackle a text beyond their immediate skills and understanding. They would not have risked this with the teacher who, in any case, would not have recommended the novel to them. Danny was able to display his expertise and ability, which he tended to downplay in the classroom, in order to maintain his status. It also seemed important for these boys to be reading together outside official literacy sessions. They were conscious of being out of reach of the teacher's assessment of their reading abilities. One of them summed up the experience as: "Well, the teacher's not around so it's sort of relaxing."

Teacher P decided that the 'trouble boys' would benefit from self-assessment in reading. He assigned them reading as a group and directed them to write evaluative comments about each other:

> (Benny) *"Jurrel read good/well and fluently but he needs to speed up. Jurrel really improved his reading and didn't laugh today."*

> (Jamel) *"Bobby read very well but he kept putting his own words into the sentences. He also needs to stop skipping words."*

> (Kerwin) *"Belvin read very well but he needs to read loud. He sometimes murmurs when he reads and sometimes he keeps reading when it's not his go but he still reads beautifully and sometimes smoothly and he always uses his hand to read along."*

> (Melvin) *"Kevin is reading good but he is not that confident on his speech. He is good at his reading but his attitude to reading is not that good, like he likes saying 'use your brains!' and it is very annoying."*

Unlike Danny's reading circle, which was entirely social in nature, this group struggled – sometimes unsuccessfully - to take responsibility for a range of difficulties in their reading: self-correction, speed, fluency, style and concentration. Teacher P responded encouragingly in their guided reading notes:

> *I am very impressed by your evaluations of your reading boys. This could be the start of something BIG! I'll make teachers of you all.*

In these different types of peer reading circles, boys were able to feel more independent about their reading, both in terms of reading choice and in self-evaluation. In both cases, teachers gave underachievers opportunities to define themselves as readers and to read together without the teacher's micro-management. For these boys, such opportunities were important markers of status, maturity and the teacher's belief in their abilities.

A new novel

In the summer term, Year 5 classes read the Louis Sachar novel, *There's A Boy in the Girls' Bathroom*.

The CLPE research team created a 'mini-journal' based on this book to see how boys would respond to writing about it in various formats over time. The mini-journal offered a series of writing and drawing prompts and invitations, linked to aspects of the story, as well as free pages for writing and drawing.

It's about a real boy who is having problems

Boys in the project were utterly engaged with this novel. It seemed to many of them very different from anything else they had ever read. It offered them ways to discuss issues of friendship and the links between self-esteem, behaviour and learning. And it was funny! Over the Summer term, children engaged in a range of independent and collaborative writing around the novel, preceded by intense discussions about the characters' actions and relationships.

For Yusuf, it was almost as if he could not believe that a book had been written about a 'real' boy who talks to his toy animals:

> *"The other books are more like kind of average and normal, or adventures and stuff like that. But this*

book is like about a real person, a boy that is having problems and he's trying to be good. ... Instead of those little dollies talking, he must be talking to himself. What Bartholomew [the bear] is saying, he is really saying to himself. He has troubles at school, he tells the dollies everything – the dollies are like a diary to him. He's trying to act tough so the other kids don't make fun of him and he doesn't get bullied."

Yusuf, like other boys who read the novel, was riveted by Bradley's evolving and sometimes intense relationship with the school's counsellor, or learning mentor, Carla:

"She is breaking through, really – thoroughly, I'm talkin about. Cause he used to be like "uh, what's up, yeah, I'm a beat you up" and stuff like that – and when he talks to Carla, after three interviews, he starts gettin better. It started when he said she was beautiful, when he said – if you was on another planet I would be ugly and you would be beautiful. She might leave him. I think he would cry when she leaves him."

Yusuf, Kenneth and all the children in Teacher K's class created their own 'Bradley's Diary,' which they also decorated in role as the protagonist.

After reading and discussing chapters of the novel, children would write daily in role as Bradley. Here Yusuf writes about how his new friend Jeff has left him to play with other boys:

Dear Diary,
Today I feel like a new boy and that is a little bit sad. Because Jeff has got new friends and he forgot about me and he is even starting to be rude to me and starting to lie like I used to. Loser! And I think in my way I am starting to improve. I think Carla likes me and I am starting to like her. Today Jeff had a black eye and he told his friends and they want to beat me up. I went in the girls' bathroom and nobody was there. The girls came. I ran into the toilet and I came out and I thought they came out and they screamed loud. (Yusuf)

Boys enjoyed writing in familiar, informal language about this novel. However, the writing in role could also be intense. Kenneth wrote a letter of advice to Bradley's on-again, off-again friend Jeff:

Jeff, man, I don't think you're doing the right thing, because all your friends used to call you Fishface and the reason they're your friends is because they feared you might give them a black eye. Bradley always used to stick up for you. Lori shouted that you went into the girls' toilet and he could have gone and told everyone but he didn't do it, he stood up for you. This is how you repay him, by leaving him and telling lies. Really you're the dumbest. One day you're going to get on Bradley's nerves and he is going to give you a black eye and your fake friends are going to leave you. All I'm saying is watch who are your real friends.

Teacher K's class had become experienced in drama work within literacy. After reading the novel, and before writing, children would hot-seat or thought track one or more of the characters. Because these forms of drama were closely linked to their reading and discussions, children had a secure understanding of how dramatic approaches to texts could help get ideas for writing – as Yusuf describes:

"Hot seating is when someone pretends to be Bradley and thinks what Bradley would say. If you ask me a question, like – 'do you like Jeff?' Bradley might say in real life "NAW", and if you asked me – 'do you like Carla?', I would say ' Forget about that, ask me the next question.' Like me, I used to be very aggressive in Year Four. I used to have a little bit of temper. It gets me more ideas, like the part when she kisses him on the cheek. I thought that was really affecting."

Book Talk: What colour is Bradley's face?

In Teacher L's class, children worked in pairs to create their own Book Talk questions which they would put to the class for discussion. This process was significant in eliciting children responses to the novel, revealing clearly that their questions, ideas and understanding could be very different from the teacher's.

Alhassan – "*Is Bradley a gangster?"*
Aaron – "*What colour is Bradley's face?"*
Victor - "*Does Bradley have an earring?"*
Christopher - "*What does Bradley do when the rest are learning?"*

In this Year 5 class, a group of boys (Caribbean Heritage and West African) argued passionately that the protagonist Bradley (in the teacher's mind, a white boy living in an all-white U.S. suburb) "must be Black" because

"He's always in trouble"
"He never cares what the teacher says"
"Because of the way everyone treats him"
"The way he is always described"
"I'm not saying all black people are troublemakers, but it's the way they talk about him in the book"
"Because he sits in the last seat in the last row of the class"

A Caribbean Heritage girl argued that "It could be that the class is all white and he is mixed race and that's why he is always alone and doesn't have any friends in the story."

Teacher L was unprepared for these ideas about Bradley's ethnicity and attributed children's comments to their lack of understanding about the novel's setting. In fact, children were bringing their own considerable background knowledge to bear in this discussion. Their interpretation of the class novel was very different from the teacher's, yet there seemed to be no framework in which to take this discussion further, or deeper. After skating across the surface of race and schooling, the talk moved on to how Bradley might be confused by his own changing behaviour:

Research officer: *Why does he tear up his homework just as he is about to put it on the teacher's desk?*

B: *He's scared.*

Research officer: *Of what?*

B: *He did it wrong, maybe it's the wrong page.*

Research officer: *But he looked at the stack of papers and it was the right page.*

B: *He's scared that it might be wrong.*

M: *He's scared that he's changing and people might start acting differently to him. He is doing different things and it scares him inside.*

K: *Inside Bradley is really good, outside he is bad. But when he changes, he's not really changing, he's bringing the inside outside.*

K: *His animals give him confidence.*

M: *It's funny but quite emotional. Because he don't get praised by other people, he makes the animals praise him. …he sort of makes them cheer for him. He's like their teacher but also some one else, like their super hero.*

J: *His animals, when no one is cheering for him, when no one likes him, the animals make him happy and make him feel better. He's pretending that the animals are people.*

K: *The animals are believing in him, saying he can do anything if he puts his mind to it.*

M: *Carla might leave because Bradley improves, and he might feel emotional and might just blank out all his good and go back to the way he was because Carla's not there to help him anymore, Carla is the one he sort of leans on and if she's not there what is he supposed to do? He might carry on being bad.*

K: *Carla might go and Bradley might be sad because she helped him through everything and supported him through everything he's done.*

B: *He might finally get his gold star and become the best student there is.*

K: *He might be angry and go back to his bad ways and do something stupid.*

In these discussions, children often mirror and re-phrase each other's comments. They propose alternative narrative paths that Bradley might take. Their talk is a children's version of the popular adult 'Book Group'. They are discussing their reading with peers, with occasional intervention from the teacher.

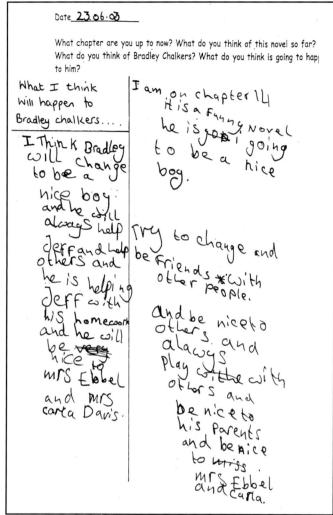

Mini-journals

Teacher L's class also wrote daily following role play, in a range of voices from the novel - as Bradley's mother, father, teacher or sister. In addition, children wrote privately about the novel in 'mini-journals' prepared by the CLPE research team. These offered a series of writing prompts and ideas as well as 'free' pages for writing and drawing.

Christopher, whose first language is Portuguese, wrote and drew enthusiastically in his mini-journal, starting with pictures of Bradley's imaginary animals and his own 'imaginary friend'.

The mini-journal was an opportunity for Christopher to engage in a wide range of writing, not all of which was assessed by his teacher. In addition to writing and performing two mini-playscripts using dialogue from the novel, Christopher also writes from his notes about the "inside" and the "outside" Bradley, following a class discussion of these differences:

> The inside of Bradley is friendly and very nice. Gentle, loves life, cares about Jeff. He likes girls. Loves his parents, loves education.

> The outside of Bradley is angry and mean. Bully, traitor, hates school, don't care about girls, unhelpful, happy, proud.

Following this, Christopher wrote, and drew, about the inside and outside, the good and bad parts, of himself:

He also writes as Bradley's father, following a discussion on a table with other boys in role as 'Mr. Chalkers':

I feel Bradley should go to military school to get some discipline. Bradley is a very nice boy but sometimes but he is a pain in the neck and a troublemaker. He broke his computer that I gave him on his birthday. Once he skipped school just to go to a game centre and he fights with his sister and sometimes when we put food on his plate he doesn't eat it - he just goes to his room and shouts and jumps on his bed.

In what might be termed his longest piece of writing, Christopher writes a never-ending list of things that come into his mind, just as Bradley does in the novel.

Wednesday 2nd July 2003

My list
Like Bradly.

- Gold Star
- Basketball.
- Football.
- School.
- Sleep.
- what does it feel to be in a wheelchair.
- home.
- car.
- Hotel.
- Swimming pool.
- what does it feel to be 40.
- Homework.
- Action Figures.
- Tv.

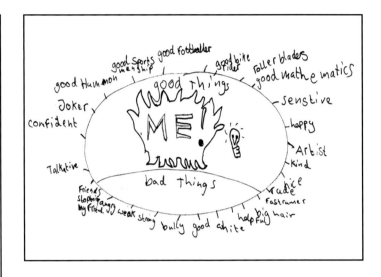

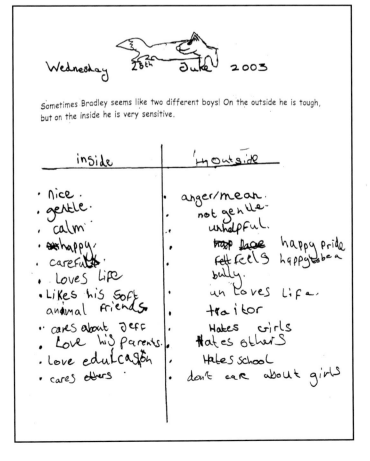

Wednesday 28th June 2003

Sometimes Bradley seems like two different boys! On the outside he is tough, but on the inside he is very sensitive.

inside	outside
nice.	anger/mean.
gentle.	not gentle.
calm	unhelpful.
happy.	face happy pride
careful.	feels happy to be a bully.
Loves life	un loves life.
Likes his soft animal friends	traitor
cares about Jeff	Hates girls
Love his parents.	Hates others
love education	Hates school
cares others	don't care about girls

My list like Bradley

Gold star
Basketball
Football
School
Sleep
What does it feel like to be in a wheelchair
Home
Car
Hotel
Swimming pool
What does it feel like to be 40
Homework
Action figures
TV
Play Station 2
Computer CD
Computer
Party
Video
Drinks/crisps
Drawing
Writing
Friends
Rival
Gameboys
Shocks
Trainers
Sings
Trousers
Jumper
Heroes
Kids
Authors
Title
Learning
Shouting
Running
Fast
Teachers
Parents
Godparents
Leaves
Trees
Boxes
Folder
Split

Christopher starts off with an item from Bradley's list: Gold stars. After that, the list morphs into things that interest Christopher: action figures, tv, cds, computers, game boy, trainers. Christopher's list casts a wide look around his own life: it covers recreation, education, family, and two questions concerned with ageing.

In the Sachar novel, Bradley says about his list, 'It's not homework. In fact, it's the opposite of homework.' Perhaps the attraction of writing lists is that it is a form of 'play' writing. List-making is an early years, emergent writing activity for young children (DfEE 2001). Boys like Christopher may be continuing patterns of emergent writing even in Year 5. List-making is a way for Christopher to play at writing in the context of a novel that deeply interests him.

Boys like Christopher, Alhassan and Yusuf became engaged in writing through a novel that interested them. The 'voice' in the novel was very much like their own voices. Hearing themselves reflected in this familiar voice was, for them, a new experience in school literacy.

Drama: It makes you actually want to come to school

Teacher L's class developed a range of dramatic vignettes from the Sachar novel. These included: using dialogue from the novel to create mini- playscripts, creating visual "thought bubbles" which were then held over characters' heads in role play, drawing story-boards of a scene and enacting these, and freeze-framing different scenes from the novel. All of these forms of enactment were performed and discussed in class.

The following piece of collaborative writing for performance involves the character Bradley listening to an angel and a devil sitting on each of his shoulders. Although Alhassan contributed very little to the writing and performance, it was a significant breakthrough for him – for a start, he got to play the Devil. The most he had previously written was his Seal Wife visualisation (page 53); his reading diary and writing folder are a series of blank pages. Alhassan is 'too cool for school'; to the annoyance of his teachers he arrives in class draped in bling (earrings, necklaces, bracelets) and declares everything to be 'boring'. His National Curriculum levels for English appear stuck at Level 2 at the end of

Year Five. As a 'can-but-don't' boy who avoids literacy at all costs, reading and writing now involve considerable risk and loss of face for Alhassan. Here, he is taking a tentative first step, playing a part and joining in school literacy. In the dialogue that follows he plays the Devil to F's Bradley and M's Angel:

Bradley: *I'm going to get that Jeff!*
Angel: *Bradley, think what you are doing.*
Bradley: *Err? What? Who's that?*
Angel: *It's your angel.*
Bradley: *Oh you, what do you want?*
Angel: *Remember Carla said everyone has good inside them and your mom said you're a good boy really.*
Bradley: *You're right.*
Devil: *Don't listen to him, he's a goody two-shoes, go up to Jeff, spit on him.*
Angel: *No that's a big sin, control yourself, please listen to me.*
Devil: *Get Jeff! Teach him a lesson! Listen to me.*
Angel: *Please Bradley think of the consequences.*
Devil: *You're tough, go get him!*
Bradley: *Please leave me alone.*
Angel: *Think about what I said.*
Devil: *I suppose you're a goody two-shoes as well.*

Enthusiasm for the novel led other boys to move beyond their reluctance to get involved with school literacy. Victor's playscript started safely, using dialogue pulled from the novel; he then felt confident enough to add his own directions, dialogue and lyrics from a song. He performed it – singing the lyrics - with Jason as Jeff:

Scene set: Outside in the playground when Jeff has a word with Bradley.
Jeff: *Hey Bradley wait up!*
(Bradley turns backwards)
Jeff: *I don't mind sitting next to you really.*
(Bradley was shocked)
Jeff: *I have really been to the White House. If you want I'll tell you about it.*
(Bradley was laughing)
Bradley: *Give me a dollar or I'll spit on you!*
(Jeff gives money and runs)
Bradley: *Money-money-money, it's a rich man's crime.*
(Bradley looks for more victims behind him)

Bradley: *If you tell the teacher I will mess up your life.*

After these performances, children discussed why they enjoyed drama. A recurring theme in discussions concerned the opportunity to play in the context of learning:

J: *"You can dance, you can act like sometimes you do, like play fighting, you do different things from normal, that's why I like drama"*

F: *"I like acting because you can move around your body, and you can learn new stories when you do it."*

K: *"You get to stand up and get out of your seats, you don't have to always be sitting and listening to Miss."*

N: *"It's fun to be other people, slouch on the table, bein' naughty."*

Drama reverses the one-way transmission mode of teaching. Children stop 'listening to Miss' and think for themselves about how to physically enter the imaginary world of the novel:

Z: *"You get to turn into a different person for a few minutes."*

M: *"When we act, we have to organise things, the way we learn who we get to be, what we have to do. We get to do things which we may never be able to do when we are older. We put words, to learn new stories, it can help you if you want to be a writer or an actor."*

Z: *"You get to work in groups, and when you work in groups you have to organise it together, so you feel like all of you have organised it, not just one person."*

These children were articulate about the aspects of drama which they valued highly. These ranged from enjoyable opportunities to get up from their seats to a heightened awareness of what and how they were learning. Children were able to reflect on how drama helped them develop effective teamwork, become active learners who are able to organise and collaborate. They

saw how 'being other people' could help them in their writing. However, some of their comments about drama perhaps reflect poorly on other parts of the literacy curriculum: "It's different from normal," "It's fun and you feel like you want to do it every day," and:

> B: "*It's usually just work in school, but now that we do something different like drama, it makes you actually WANT to come to school.*"

Emailing Bradley

Children in Teacher S's class entered the world of this contemporary novel by emailing the main character, Bradley Chalkers. Boys enthusiastically wrote emails to this 'trouble boy', as well as to his Learning Mentor Carla and his sister Claudia. It was writing that boys felt they owned, and it was 'real' writing. Once again, the CLPE research team set up an email address for Bradley, and the project researcher would return children's emails in role. Teacher S reported: "The emails are amazing, they can't believe it when they get a response."

Andrew spent his entire 'Golden Time' (a period of free-choice activity which children earn for good behaviour) writing this email; it was writing that he actively wanted to do. As his teacher observed, Andrew had never before chosen to use his Golden Time for writing:

> *Dear Bradley*
> *Thank you for replying and answering my questions. So you think you're cool. I think you are but I'm cooler. Trust me, you have trouble with girls, well you shouldn't. In my school I've got all the girls calling my name and no offence but I've never been beaten up by a girl. All of them are shy but in your school I'd probably have one purple and one black eye!*
>
> *Trust me Carla won't make fun of you and don't listen to your sister when she says that that's just Carla's job. Carla is just like you, as both of you are trying to make friends. I bet you are going errr! Is this boy mad? But I'm not. Why do think you both like odd socks.*

My favourite part in the novel is when you kept saying 'call the doctor if you don't believe me' it made the whole class laugh people could not sit still.

Here are some facts if you want to have a good image:
- *First: have a bath every day*
- *Secondly: hide your odd socks or try and wear matching ones*
- *Thirdly: were a strong breath-taking after shave*
- *Fourth: take part in a sport and play for the school*
- *Fifth: make friends with a small little quiet boy, maybe a girl*
- *These are my facts. I hope you use them.*
- *From the one and only Master of the net Andrew*

Yours sincerely
P.S. Your sister is diabolical

Jermaine and Sofiya wrote to Carla, the learning mentor, or counsellor. After showing their considerable knowledge of events in the novel, they asked questions as a way of speculating about what might happen to Bradley. In their questions, Jermaine and Sofiya were using their Book Talk skills:

Dear Carla,
Hi our names are Jermaine and Sofiya we are writing to you to say a big thank you for all your help. We really appreciate what you are doing for Bradley but we would like to tell you that Bradley has lied to you about a couple of stuff.
He has lied to you about him and Jeff splitting up Bradley has lied to you about the black eye. The truth was Colleen done it.
He even lied to you about the presidents' hats.
He lied about him not allowed to speak.

We would really want you to be our councilor and give us advice about our problems. We think you're a really good councilor and pretty because you don't look at yourself but you think about others. You have feelings for others. We have seen what Bradley gets up to so we've made a list for you to discuss with him.

Homework
Persuade him to get stars
Be polite
Stop fighting with girls
Listen to the teacher carefully
Not to lie!!!

We have gave you a couple of things we would like you to discuss with him and we are hoping that these things will come true. I would like to tell you something what Bradley done. He ripped his list. We would like to ask you some questions from us.

Do you think Bradley will be successful with this list?
Do you think Bradley and Jeff will be friends again?
We like your personality but what do you think about Bradley's?
We hope Bradley will [have] success by all your advice and help.

Gus and Kwaku wrote to Bradley's sister Claudia, in no uncertain terms, using capital letters for emphasis:

Dear Claudia,
Why are you teasing Bradley? Would you like it if everyone teased you? You need a serious lesson in manners. Are you jealous or something? I think it's time you needed a councillor. You are mean, unpleasant and unfair. How did you know about the list that he made? You pick on Bradley and now you are in serious trouble! IF YOU WANT TO PICK ON SOMEONE, PICK ON SOMEONE YOUR OWN SIZE!!! Why are you stepping on Bradley's animals just because you don't have any friends? As soon as you get this email, tell your mum and dad you are picking on Bradley. THINK ABOUT WHAT I AM SAYING! Tell Bradley to email me and you are going to get a serious disipline. You need to spend more time on your Maths, English and science. I am hiring you a teacher and he will work from 4.00pm to 6.00pm,
Monday to Sunday.
Has that given you a lesson?
From Gus and Kwaku

Children in this class were all performing the same writing task: emailing a character in the novel. Their responses, however, were wide-ranging in content and in style. As they entered the world of the novel, they each had their own ideas, advice and questions to put to the fictional characters. Merchant (2003) has described email as a combination of face-to-face interaction and written communication. The emails to Bradley, and to Lulu, show children grasping both of these modes with enthusiasm. Underachievers had no difficulties in generating this imaginative writing, they were no longer staring at a blank page unable to get ideas,

Evaluations

This was a text that mesmerised many boys in the project. When the project researcher visited school B, a group of boys raced across the playground to exclaim: "We're reading this BOOK called *There's a Boy in the Girls' Bathroom*!" and they literally begged their teacher to read more of it every day. Teacher P's 'trouble boys' reading group wrote in their reading notes:

> B: "*We think this book is funny and quite good and I think that our group should read more books like this. And our group read with expression and we really like this book a lot.*"

> J: "*I think the book is hilarious.*"

Aaron made his mother buy two other novels by the same author – and he stole *There's a Boy in the Girls' Bathroom* from Teacher L (who subsequently got it back). The teacher told the project researcher: *Aaron has not had a very good year – the only thing that has motivated him is this book.*

Teacher K reported: "Parents keep coming in saying – what is this book he keeps going on about?" She also had to admit that reading the novel made her think differently about where she seats boys in the classroom:

"*Rammone is Bradley, and I'm just like that awful teacher in the book Mrs. Ebble because I make him sit "in the last seat in the last row". And now I think he's noticed that.*"

Yusuf's mother told the project researcher: "He has never been interested in reading before, except for this book. It's all he talks about at home now."

Teaching literacy using a contemporary text gave many boys opportunities to discuss, enact and write about many issues that mattered to them: bullying, being cool, being tough, being scared, friendship and betrayal. The fact that Bradley was tough outside, but vulnerable inside, may have given this text a special appeal for them. Some ethnic minority boys clearly saw many of their experiences reflected in the novel. For some boys, it was the first time they had actively wanted to read and their first enthusiasm for a particular author.

Teachers provided many different opportunities for children to respond to the novel: drama, discussion, writing in role, mini-journals and emails. It was a text that offered ways into literacy through its contemporary content, but its success was also related to teachers' willingness to engage with the full range of children's responses. Boys who wrote continuously, in mini-journals or diaries, began to develop more stamina for writing, and in some cases their transcription improved through this daily writing.

Although the novel was 'assigned' reading, boys in the project responded as if the book had been a matter of personal choice. For underachievers this was a high-status novel which they could read independently. Boys talked about the novel at home, and they talked about it in school. In their discussions, they became communities of readers. They wanted to read other novels by the same author. They chose to take risks and extend their writing. They wanted to perform their writing. And they began to engage in the social networking around texts that supports effective literacy learning.

7

WRITING PROCESSES AND PRODUCTS:

PATTERNS OF TEACHING THAT MADE A DIFFERENCE

drama to improve writing even though not on writing

Although this was not purely a 'writing' project, the interventions made by the project – which included the use of specific texts for discussion, drama and ICT work - were intended to engage targeted boys in literacy and to improve the quality of their writing. The amount of time that was spent in different classrooms on these interventions varied, as did the continuity of the teaching. Therefore, the three specific texts introduced, and their associated writing tasks, engaged boys to a greater or lesser degree. These differences were reflected in the extent of the improvements which were perceived in boys' writing.

The interventions introduced by CLPE emphasised approaches to literacy which made writing a social rather than a solitary activity. Drama and performance around texts highlighted the importance of audience and of communication. Collaboration, peer support, discussion and different forms of planning made the writing process more explicit to underachievers. Using ICT for imaginative and factual writing engaged boys' interest and expertise. In classrooms where writing was developed as a form of 'engagement in social action' (Applebee 2000), boys began to change their behaviour as writers spontaneously. Patterns of improvement in writing emerged across the six Key Stage 2 classrooms.

what about the girls? was teens not encouraged as well?

Parts to whole: the power of collaboration

Where teachers created frequent and sustained opportunities for children to write collaboratively, underachievers' participation in the collaborative process supported their development as writers. This collaborative process provided underachievers with models of cohesive, whole-text writing whereas working alone they struggled to generate and sustain their writing.

One area of improvement in independent writing can be seen in the paragraphs of 'visualisation' that children in Teacher L's class wrote from the Seal Wife story. The short pieces showed some indicators of increasing sophistication and experience in writing, as described in Barrs & Cork (2001:189). These indicators include the appearance of mental state verbs, which take readers into characters' thoughts and emotions, the presence of echoes of the original story and the use of literary language.

The waves crashed dangerously close to her. I was terrified she might do something silly. I was

wondering what she was doing. There was a man in the water, I don't know who he was but he had seal skin like my mum. He was trying to pull her in the water. The weather was very corrupt, there was lightening and it stopped me because it was very loud. My mum jumped in the water. I was in despair. I went up to my bed and never forgot her again.
(Aaron: an ending to the Seal Wife story)

However, the writing undertaken in this and in other classrooms tended to be fragmentary: beginnings, endings, pivotal moments, or writing briefly in role:

For my darling children, I will miss you so much. I can not come back. I'm very sorry your dad and I wed. Your dad forced me to stay. It was like a prison. That is because he stole my seal skin. It's nearly morn. I love you, Mum.
(Danny: a letter from the Seal Wife to her children)

These powerful fragments never grow into complete texts. The growing use of written language forms and of literary language is apparent (*your dad and I wed; it's nearly morn; the waves crashed dangerously close*) but the

fragments exist in a vacuum. There is no attempt at making a whole, cohesive text or at writing beyond the single paragraph. In some cases, teachers felt driven by timetables to move on to other literacy work; others felt unsure how to develop these fragments into longer pieces of writing. Developing writers therefore had no support for moving towards writing sustained, whole texts.

The same indicators of growing experience and sophistication in writing were seen in the collaborative seal stories in Teacher G's Year 4 class. These texts were subsequently performed to the class and videotaped (page 60). Unlike weaker writers in other classes who were working independently, these collaborative groups of writers are able - sometimes imperfectly - to create whole texts. In the passage that follows, we see Wilfred, Ertan and Okierete retelling the seal wife story, working together on a large sheet of paper.

Wilfred, ERTAN and <u>Okierete,</u>
(* = echo of the original text)

Once upon a time a man called McCodrum went / <u>trudged</u> *along the (golden sand beachcombing *). He spotted some* <u>shining</u> *seals playing by the sea.* <u>They</u> / *slowly* /<u>crawled along the shore and pulled off their skins and turned into beautiful woman.</u>

<u>One woman was more pretty than the others. Then he said to himself.</u> *"I love this girl,* she looks lovely". <u>He seized the seal skin and hid it behind his back. The seal woman said "Give it back"/</u>

GIVE IT BACK NOW OR I WILL CALL THE POLICE ON YOU!

When MacCodrum got home he hunted for a secret place to hide the skin. WHILE THE SEAL WOMAN WAS LOOKING FOR MACCODRUM, HE WAS HIDING FROM HER. <u>Then she found him. "What are you doing?" she asked. "Nothing", he said,</u> *thinking that she would not find her skin.*

EVERY NIGHT HER FRIENDS SHOUTED LISA, LISA COME BACK, WE NEED YOU PLEASE.

The little kid said "Mum what was that dad took from the rafters?" "What was it like?" the mum said. It was like a golden sparkling beautiful seal skin. IT WAS SEAL SKIN ALLRIGHT.

Alright. (I will leave you for a while *). <u>Every day she left fish for her beloved children.</u>

The next morning the children dashed into their mother's empty, silent room but she was not to be found. They searched the whole house but they did not find her one bit. They checked the whole sea (the whole ocean). They began to panic.

They were yelling, "Mother, Mother. Where are you?" They were shouting over the whole ocean.

"However, are we going to find her?"

As they grew older they began to think they were going to enjoy the outside life but something strange started to happen to them. Whenever the twins saw their reflections in the sparkling sea they notices that they had sprouted fins. They felt terrified but weird. They wanted to be normal like everyone else.

They decided to try out some swimming in the bright ocean. They plunged into the foaming waves. They swam past the friendly seals and crashed into one with the most beautiful furry coat. As she was knocked over her beautiful skin dropped and they noticed it was their mother. Oh how they were glad to see her. They cuddled her and one of them said, " We want to turn back to normal."

"OK" replied their mother. " YOU must look deeply into the shining full moon through a hagstone and make your wish to turn back to normal." And that is what they did!

A wonderful story written as a team. *what is good about people get a chance to read.*

Collaboration gives weaker writers like Okieriete opportunities to contribute ideas to the text and experience the creation of a whole story. Okieriete said that 'trudged' was a better word than 'went' because "It's more like how he was actually walking because he was lonely". He uses the literary words "seized" and "beloved" which recur in readings of the story. Wilfred adds "slowly" to the phrase about the seals' crawling. He lets readers into the fisherman's thoughts (*thinking she would not find her skin*) and he recalls the words of the story in two places. Ertan contributes the more exciting and direct *Give it back now or I will call the police on you!* to the seal woman's speech. As Goodwin (1999) has observed in other classroom contexts, these writers achieve much more together than they would on their own. They also see the writing process 'in action' as they cross out, change, insert or add words on the large paper.

But their story does not make sense. Readers must have background knowledge to fill in the gaps in their text; a central chunk of the narrative is missing in which the seal woman lives with the fisherman and has children, the *little kid* of their story. These novice writers have the story in their heads, but it isn't all there on paper. The writing is cohesive within paragraphs but not between paragraphs. Through performance readings of their stories, these gaps were made more apparent to the authors. This provided a clear focus for subsequent teaching and for writing targets.

Babah, KENNY, Darren and Hinga wrote a more sophisticated continuation of the Seal Wife story, describing the fate of the Seal Wife's children. This collaborative text was written over several days, with additions and changes to words and phrases and a closer focus on punctuation. When they came to perform their story, one of the boys wore a long wig to indicate he was the seal mother. Dialogue was read by the narrator and echoed by the actors. The 'hagstone' in the story refers to the practice in this class of telling stories around in a circle: whoever was narrating would hold a 'magic stone'.

The next morning, the children went / ran / dashed *into their mother's* empty, silent *room,* BUT SHE WAS NOT TO BE FOUND. *They searched the whole house but they did not find her /* one bit. *They checked the whole sea,* the whole ocean. *They began to panic. They were* saying / yelling (")*Mother Mother where are you* (?") THEY SHOUTED (over) THE WHOLE OCEAN (") *How ever are we going to find her* (?")

As they grew older they began to think they were going *to enjoy the outside life.* But *something strange started to happen to them. Whenever the twins saw their reflections in the sparkling sea they* NOTICED THAT THEY HAD SPROUTED FINS.

They felt terrified but weird. THEY WANTED TO BE NORMAL LIKE EVERYONE ELSE. *They decided to try out some swimming in the* shiny, bright *ocean. They plunged in the foaming waves.* They swam past the friendly seals *and bumped* / CRASHED *into one with the most beautiful* furry coated *seal.*

As she was knocked over her beautiful skin opened / dropped *and they noticed it was their mother.* Oh how they were glad to see her. *They hugged* / cuddled *her and* ONE OF THEM *said* "We want to turn back to normal". "OK" REPLIED THEIR MOTHER "You must look deeply into the shining full moon, through a hagstone and make your wish to turn back to normal"

And that is what they did.

The Freaky End

Collaboration improves this already coherent and cohesive text as the writers brainstorm more sophisticated vocabulary: *went* becomes *dashed, saying* becomes *yelling,* and the weak *bumped* becomes the more violent *crashed.* Sentences are extended: *They dashed into their mother's empty, silent room but she was not to be found.* The characters' feelings are described and made more explicit: *They felt terrified but weird. They wanted to be normal like everyone else.* These writers were also able to hear where appropriate punctuation should be, as they re-read their story aloud.

In negotiating and building these texts, one at beginner level and one at a more advanced level, children's writing develops in vocabulary and in complexity. The writers echo their reading in words and phrases. Often one writer continues when another runs out of ideas, so sentences become more complex. In both examples, the writing process is more spontaneous than planned. These boys are literally shaping their writing "at the point of utterance" (Britton 1980: 65); they *speak* their writing as they construct the text aloud.

In independent writing, ideas in the writer's head become words on paper. Collaboration makes this process explicit. Writers working together must articulate their ideas and words before writing them down. As they do so, they continuously evaluate and reflect on their developing text.

Collaboration can be a powerful framework in which weaker writers develop expertise – but it also may be initially frustrating because it slows down the writing

process. Writers must listen to each other and incorporate different ideas in their text, they must select the most appropriate words and phrases, decide what comes next and how to conclude a piece of writing. It is in these negotiating spaces where children may 'see the writing process develop' (Graves 1983: 219) as they pursue a pattern of 'select, compose, read, select, compose, read'.

The teachers' management of this process, and children's ability to negotiate and collaborate, required skills which were emphasised by the intervention made at the very beginning of the project, when each class devised its own 'Rules for Talk.' Without awareness and experience of talk and negotiation *in the context of literacy,* these children would not have been able to collaborate so effectively as writers.

In the collaborative process, weaker writers who would otherwise struggle alone to generate, control and sustain their ideas on paper see the big shape of a complete text as they contribute to it. Their understanding of how the text makes sense is reinforced in performance by reading aloud. They have a basis for moving on to independent writing.

The research team observed that many children in Teacher P's classroom demonstrated considerable stamina for writing independently and at length, and speculated that this could have been developed by their extensive experience of collaborative writing during the previous year in Teacher G's class.

ICT as 'play' writing and real writing for underachievers

Email was another form of collaborative writing which was usually done in pairs. This was due to the numbers of computers in a suite, or to teachers trying to ensure equal access to the single class computer. Where teachers created opportunities for children to email the fictional characters Lulu or Bradley in response to Charles Causley's poem and Louis Sachar's novel, boys displayed perseverance and intense interest in this form of literacy.

Teachers reported children's amazement and even disbelief at receiving responses to their emails. In emailing fictional characters, boys would imaginatively and enthusiastically enter the world of the texts: it was both 'play' and 'real' writing, imaginary and yet linked to real world experiences of literacy (for instance, letter-writing or texting). Boys may be less experienced at the 'play' writing that girls engage in from their early years. This lack of experience may become a real disadvantage when boys reach Key Stage Two and are required to take on a wide range of roles in different writing genres: story-teller, advertiser, historian, scientist.

Email was writing that underachievers could own at both the macro (text content) and micro (spelling, punctuation) levels. Where teachers wanted boys to take more responsibility for transcription, they would engage the Word programme's red line/green line so that boys could independently correct errors in spelling and punctuation.

Underachievers in this project benefited from experiences of literacy that allowed them to play at reading and writing without appearing 'babyish'. The interventions involving ICT, such as email, software to stimulate discussion, screen and web reading and web publishing, were all high-status ways for underachievers to practise reading and writing. Boys who shunned literacy work were drawn into writing emails:

> Teacher S: *What are you two doing?*
> T & G: *We're emailing Bradley. His worst subject is language. Our worst subject is literacy. We hate literacy.*
> Teacher: *But what you're doing is literacy!*
> T & G: *No it's not.*
> Teacher: *Yes it is – you're writing!*
> T & G: *This is different writing.*

Technology has changed the way children perceive and experience literacy (Goetze 2002) by making it both more purposeful and, importantly, more playful. If email is both real and play writing, perhaps real and play *reading* for many children now involves multimedia, games and web reading. As a Year 5 teacher was demonstrating an educational CD ROM to a visitor, one child whispered: "Look, they're playing Ancient Greeks!" Not reading, but 'playing'. In classrooms where boys are rejecting the offered curriculum, but appear to respond positively to learning with computers, this may be because ICT offers opportunities for children to *play* in a real-world literacy context.

Merchant (2003) has argued that email "promotes the culturally valued practices of reading and writing," and that ignoring this form of communication could increase the polarisation of in-school and out-of-school literacy practices. The electronic interactions of reading, writing and responding around the Causley poem and the Sachar novel in this project enriched children's experiences of these texts. Using ICT to read, write and communicate beyond the classroom added a new dimension to literacy.

Generating enthusiasm with drama

After they had physically entered the imaginary world of the text through role play or enactment, boys' independent writing would often begin to pick up on the registers of the text, recall its turns of phrase, and echo the voices of the characters themselves. In Teacher L's class, the impact that the 'intervention' texts made on children's writing was especially noticeable among those boys with English as an additional language.

> *My son is a very nice and gentle boy but you just don't give him the chance to show that, because I know that inside of him he won't harm a fly. Bradley is a very good boy and if you give my Bradley a chance he'll show you what kind of person he is, and then you'll see the real Bradley my son, because I don't want my little baby Bradley to go to military school.*
> (Murad, Arabic speaker, as Mrs. Chalkers)

> *Look what I draw: it's a nightmare. I am the best at drawing in the world. Last week I got an A in maths, literacy, art and spelling. I never lie. I'm the big boss. I'm rich like Beckham. I've got so many friends – everybody in the world loves me like a king.*
> (Jason, Portuguese speaker, as Bradley)

> *Dear Mrs. Ebbel, I think Bradley is an overgrown baby and he lies too much and he always gets me and his mum in the middle of it. He spits like javelins on the sports day track, so I think he should go to military school. From: Mr. Chalkers. PS: Phone me when something bad happens because he won't tell me.*
> (Victor, Yoruba speaker, as Mr. Chalkers)

Boys wrote enthusiastically following drama or role play around all three texts, the poem, the short story and the novel. Where teachers focused on characters and character development (as in Teacher L's class), writers were able to imagine more fully what characters would say and how they would say it. Where teachers focused on visualising and 'walking around' a scene or a setting (the Seal stories in Teacher S's class, or Lulu's Room in Teacher P's class), writers were able to imagine and write in detail about the world of their text. Through drama, children write in imaginary voices. Graves (1983: 219) describes voice as the mainspring of powerful writing:

> Voice is the imprint of ourselves on our writing. It is that part of the self that pushes the writing ahead, the dynamo in the process. Take the voice away and the writing collapses of its own weight. There is no writing, just words following words.

For these underachievers, enthusiasm for drama was also the first step in increasing the *quantity* of their writing. In classrooms where children were given opportunities to write at length and write complete texts, this enthusiasm led to increasing stamina for writing. However, in other contexts, teachers' initial excitement at the voices and registers appearing in children's writing after drama work turned to disappointment when these improvements were not sustained in longer pieces of writing. As noted earlier, this lack of development was most apparent in classrooms where children consistently wrote fragments and paragraphs rather than whole texts.

The presence of others

Where teachers habitually brought children's writing together for a whole class reading or performance (such as teacher P's 'Seal Wife in Divorce Court'), weaker writers could experience the overarching text and begin to understand how an extended text 'hangs together', even if they could not yet manage this independently. This form of collaboration, somewhat like a patchwork quilt, was helpful to developing writers, who could add their own small patch to the fabric of the whole text.

Knowledge that writing would be performed or published motivated both groups and individuals to persevere with their writing. When the purpose of writing was to publish, perform or read it to an audience, the writing was better. As Jermaine said of his Seal Story that he read to younger children in school:

> "The things I've written and published it, not really published but read to people and get their opinion how it is I can improve stories, what they've said that's good about it, what they've said that bad about it, and the NEXT story that I do I can improve that bit about it and keep the good bits and make it even gooder."

Arendt (1958) said that "For excellence, the presence of others is always required". These 'others' may be in cyberspace as well as in the classroom, and the virtual audience of the project website was equally as motivating to writers as the audience of school. Like ICT, performance can inject both play and purpose into to the English curriculum. On the evidence of boys' writing and behaviour in this project, a strong case can be made for teachers to use more audience-oriented strategies in literacy.

Time to talk, think and then write

Children's writing showed increasing thought and imagination where teachers approached writing through discussions of reading - with the whole class, in small groups, in the computer suite, at the class computer, with editing partners or in literature circles. This took time, but the amount of time underachieving boys had to discuss, develop and revise their ideas had a direct impact on the quantity and quality of their writing.

In classes where children moved between discussion and writing over time in order to create and publish a complete 'product' (such as the Seal story books in Teacher S's class), children were able to grow and refine their ideas and address issues such as spelling and punctuation separately from composition. Where children had time to write complete texts, these texts were both coherent (in that they made sense) and cohesive (they showed linkage between paragraphs and within paragraphs). The writers in Teacher S's class were able to experience the whole writing process, from the initial germ of an idea to the public reading of a finished, designed story book.

Oral rehearsal and increasing control of standard English

Where boys' writing developed as a consequence of extended opportunities for retelling, text enactment and role play, their written texts showed increasing control of standard English forms. Oral rehearsal gave them practice in trying out literary language and increased their confidence in using it.

In the 1970s, research in inner London schools (such as the 1974 Vauxhall Talk Workshop) looked at how standard English may be a second language for many native English speakers. The differences between standard forms and urban or ethnic vernaculars, such research suggested, could be made explicit to non-standard speakers through talk, drama and performance. Three decades on in the present project, boys' spoken language – their home dialect - continues to be a strong feature of their writing in school, e.g;

Zak: "*He saw something what he thought would change his life forever.*"

Kwaku: "*He never knew no one.*"

Omar: "*Somethink was itching him.*"

Daniel: "*He wanted to take her seal skin and he done that.*"

Jason: "*She tod me that she lef but she will member me.*"

Jermaine: "*He lived by his self... The ladies was wearing long dresses.*"

Kenneth: "*He sat in the big lever chair.*"

Kenneth: "*I have a nover husben.*"

Of course, oral language is a significant aspect of who we are. Research in secondary schools documents how boys much more than girls (Hewitt 1990) deliberately acquire and speak non-standard English as an act of adolescent identity. The observation that adult women tend to use more 'prestige' language forms than men is discussed in Gordon (1997) and Cameron & Coates (1988). In the years of upper primary school, boys' developing identity may also express itself through language and in a resistance to school literacy with its use of conventional standard English. Perhaps because girls are more experienced at taking on a variety of roles in imaginary play, they write more fluently in standard

English as one of many 'roles' – and this impacts on their attainment scores.

Ann Williams (1989 and 2001) has documented the influence of home dialects on a wide range of grammatical forms and accent-related spelling in children's writing. Roxy Harris (1995) has described these as 'fragments and fractures' between speech and writing, and has observed that adults as well as child learners show 'regular and consistent signs' of oral language varieties of English in their writing:

It is true that natural speakers of Standard English also have to make adjustments in moving from speech to writing. I would suggest, though, that the adjustments are far fewer than for those whose normal spoken language is not Standard English. I would further suggest that there has been an under-estimation in education of the subtle difficulties of adjustment for very many learners faced with these issues.

Kenneth's seal story, which follows, illustrates the difficulties that many children face in writing standard English. Through reading, enactment and discussion, he is beginning to use literary language forms, and language from the story, in his own writing. However, his spelling and his sentence construction are both heavily influenced by vernacular English.

I turned around to discover a man rushing at me, I ran as quickly as my legs could caring to get my seal skin but to my surprise, the man had seal skin in his hands. As I look up to his face I sobbed for my skin but all he said, "This is the greatest catch, this I will keep". He grabbed my wrist and taken me to the cottage, living me to seat and wornder about my seal life. He left at lest ten minutes. He came back emyte handed. So I knew he hedit. As time went by I grew to love him but always miss seal family. Soon we got married and we had free children. Their names were Tommy, Jo, and Lulu. One day I let the children play out near the haystack. And to my children surprise back from the haystack there something fellout. They came runny at me. They screamed "Mummy what's this?" As I grab Tommy Jo and Lulu and I kiss their head, I took the seal skin. I ran trelled water, fell down my face. I jumped into to the water and shouted fellwell.

Kenneth's use of speech structures in his writing influences his spelling strategies, e.g:

- *he hedit*
- *free children*
- *they came runny at me*
- *I grab Tommy (for 'grabbed')*
- *I kiss their head (for 'kissed')*
- *fell down my face (missing 'on')*

However, through the sustained oral work around texts going on in his class, written language structures are emerging:

- *I turned around to discover a man rushing at me*
- *I ran as quickly as my legs could caring (carry)*
- *I sobbed for my skin*
- *"This is the greatest catch, this I will keep"* (echo of story text)
- *He came back emyte handed (empty-handed)*
- *I jumped into the water and shouted fellwell* (farewell)

The problems in Kenneth's writing arise from the tension between the spoken and the written language forms, as he struggles to control the myriad aspects of the writing process: ideas and overall coherence, genre and narrative structure, spelling and punctuation, grammar and sentence construction. As Warren & Gillborn (2003) have noted in their wider research, the National Strategies may be inadequate to address the needs of learners such as Kenneth, who are - it is important to note - not new arrivals to the English education system. As many teachers will know, boys who write like Kenneth are not unusual.

As teachers noted in interviews, they often felt unsure about using oral rehearsal for writing because there were no immediate, markable outcomes from it. However, since we can demonstrate the influence of non-standard spoken varieties of English on children's writing, we have to ask how teaching might most effectively address the issue of helping children to take on standard written English.

Experienced teachers in the project did this readily. Through talk, discussion, reading aloud, drama, role play and performance, they and the children were able to explore language differences and make them explicit. Teacher G talked frankly with children about the differences between 'posh' and 'normal' speech, both in whole class discussions and separately with groups of boys using the computer spell-check, often making the point that "a lot of writing can seem like posh speaking." In these classes, children such as Kenneth showed increasing language awareness, and this influenced their choice of language in oral rehearsal and in writing.

Flexible formats to organise ideas

Where teachers offered different ways for children to think about and organise their ideas before writing, boys showed increased motivation for writing. During the two terms of the project, teachers worked successfully with different types of drafting and planning:

- Visualisation and mind-mapping (Teacher S)
- Overnight thinking time (Teachers L and K)
- Moving from a large-scale collaborative draft to small-scale final copy (Teachers G and P)

Open-ended planning such as overnight thinking time, mind-mapping, collaborative editing and discussion helped many boys to see a clear progression from their plan and their draft to their final piece of writing. These facilitating structures encouraged note-taking, talking to others in and outside of school, and 'big-shape' thinking about the meaning of the whole developing text. They moved boys away from writing a draft and then copying it out, what Okiereiete called "having to write it and write it again." or Jermaine described as "having to write it and write it."

Large-scale formats for collaborative drafting made a difference to targeted Year 4 boys' motivation during the writing process. When groups of children had the option of recording their initial ideas on A3 (or larger) paper using large felt-tip pens, making changes and additions in different colours, boys' motivation to write was sustained simply because these drafts were so much easier to read and edit. The large-scale format was colourful and friendly – children also liked to draw pictures on these drafts – and there was an element of 'play' in this kind of writing. Large formats also freed up the physical act of writing for boys whose fine motor skills were still in development. Okieriete said, "I used to cramp my writing;" his handwriting improved with the introduction of large-format drafting and he became more motivated to re-draft. Ashley began to write more in the large format because "I can see what I'm doing, it's easy to put things in and take things out, plus I can read my writing better." .

Opportunities to draw in their writing also increased motivation. Year 5 children expressed disbelief at Teacher S 'allowing' them to draw in their writing books. Underachievers at Key Stage Two may be continuing patterns of early stages in writing develop-ment by weaving drawing into their writing to convey or emphasise meaning. (Dyson 1988), Bearne (2002) finds that boys like to make use of images to structure their writing. This was certainly true for Jermaine, who used a pictorial writing plan, whose illustrations mark each transition and each new chapter in the text, and who says his story reminds him of what he's seen on television and in films.

Finally, improvements in boys' writing over two terms were usually triggered by enthusiasm of some kind - for a text, for story-telling, for drama, for using interactive ICT, for a new kind of planning. As teachers have observed in the Reading and Writing Projects in the Local Education Authority of Croydon (Graham 1999, 2003), putting 'fun' into literacy teaching inevitably engenders a positive response from children.

From transmission to interaction

Patterns of teaching that highlighted the active, social dimension of writing through discussion, communication, collaboration and performance created openings for boys to become more involved in school literacy. Oral rehearsal also created new openings for teachers.

Introducing the story of The Seal Wife, Teacher S reported that for the first time she had told a story to her class without reading it from a book:

"It was the first time I ever just told a story to them without reading it. It was amazing - the eye contact with them. I had never done that before. So intense."

Following her oral story-telling of 'The Seal Wife,' Teacher L asked children (after overnight thinking time) to come to class prepared to tell their own stories, about themselves:

"And I found out a lot of things about them, things I never knew before. It was the first time I just listened to them talking."

At a CLPE conference on 'Writing and the Imagination' (Steele 2004), drama lecturer Susanna Steele expressed concern that "the language of the class-room is predominantly transactional, instructive and related to the ongoing activities of the classroom." She argued that hearing the expressive language of literature is crucial to children's development as readers and writers, and that "All the exercises; the reminders about the ingredients of a good story; the model text; the word banks; the good openings; powerful verbs; 'interesting adjectives' do not create a literary 'reservoir' for children to draw on. Many children are being asked to write in drought conditions." In this project, where teachers made time for children's talk to flourish around a powerful text, children were able to use that talk in the service of their writing. Teachers in turn had time to observe and assess children's language and consider how to further their literacy development.

8

MAKING PROGRESS
IN WRITING

Individual boys were observed over two terms and a range of their writing was collected before, during and after the interventions carried out for the project. Written texts collected were very different in context, genre and content. They included independent and collaborative writing, diaries, stories, letters, emails and scripts for performances.

Tools to track improvement

The CLPE Writing Scale for ages 8 to 12 (page 26) was used to assess boys' progress as writers. Teachers judged progress on this Scale by assessing children's writing behaviour and by sampling a collection of writing over time. An additional list of writing competences emerged in the course of the project, based on the writing samples and on observations of children as writers. These competences – *Characteristics of Improving Writers* and *Characteristics of Improving Writing* (see below) – detailed the changes in writing behaviour of focus boys and improvements in their writing over the two terms of the project.

As a result of the project interventions, focus boys showed changes in their behaviour as writers. These changes were characteristic of developing writers and were conceptualised on a continuum from increasing confidence and stamina for writing to increasing independence and experience in writing. These aspects of progress were interrelated: confidence, stamina, experience and independence hinged upon increasing involvement and engagement in the writing process.

As a result of their increasing involvement in literacy and increasing confidence, boys were writing at more length and acquiring more experience as writers. As they did so, their writing began to include more features of written language forms and to echo literary language. With their increasing stamina as writers, their writing became more sustained and controlled. And as they became more confident and independent in their writing, what they wrote became more ambitious and complex in character.

In this analysis of writing, therefore, boys' behaviour was taken into account as a factor in their improvement as writers. By looking for evidence of changes in their behaviour as writers as a result of the interventions, and at how these changes impacted on the writing itself, it was possible to reconceptualise 'failing' writers as 'improving' writers. Boys who wrote very little were beginning to take risks and write more. Boys who were unenthusiastic about writing ('can-but-don't' writers) were becoming more engaged. Boys who had 'loads of ideas' but serious technical problems were learning to control their writing better. It was observable that where teachers succeeded in creating an environment that inspired children to write, boys began to change their behaviour as writers.

Characteristics of improving writers

Increasing confidence and independence
- less reluctant to write
- more willing to take risks
- needing less teacher support
- more self-starting

Increasing involvement
- more engaged
- more self-motivated
- gaining more satisfaction from writing
- more able to take on another viewpoint and voice

Increasing experience and stamina
- writing at more length
- concentrating for longer periods
- tackling a wider range of texts

Increasing range of strategies
- more able to plan writing, including use of non-linear forms (eg mind-maps)
- more able to work effectively with a writing partner
- more able to self-correct writing (including spelling)

Increasing knowledge and understanding
- increasing understanding of the structures of written language
- more aware of genres and literary forms

Increasing ability to reflect
- more able to discuss and develop their writing
- engaging in self assessment

Characteristics of improving writing

Language
- language moves away from writing close to speech and uses written language forms and structures
- language shows evidence of texts that have been read
- language appropriate to genre and purpose

Length and complexity
- texts become longer, ideas more sustained
- texts show increasing syntactic complexity

Coherence and cohesion
- texts more coherent and make more sense
- texts more cohesive between paragraphs

Control of aspects of narrative writing
- world of text more fully imagined
- characterisation more fully developed
- evidence of control of dialogue in narration

Reader and audience
- texts show growing awareness of reader and sense of audience

Punctuation and spelling
- texts marked for meaning with appropriate punctuation
- texts show range of spelling strategies and standard forms

Conditions and criteria for good writing

In all but a few cases, National Curriculum writing levels and CLPE writing scale results for boys in the project were lower than their levels and scale results for reading (page 24). The reading abilities of boys in the project were good; yet only seven of the 24 focus boys were above National Curriculum Attainment Level 2 in Writing at the start of the project. This was something that puzzled and frustrated teachers. Since many of these boys enjoyed reading, why did the connections that learners make between reading and writing (Meek in Barrs & Cork 2001) not seem to be working for them?

Low attainment in writing may be linked to an underdeveloped reading culture. As noted in Chapter 6, the reading environment in most classrooms was limited, and most of the teachers had not been using whole texts as part of their teaching of literacy. For four of the six teachers, the interventions introduced by the project represented the first time they had used a whole text (short story or novel) for literacy teaching. Boys were reading at home, but their reading was not always being encouraged or developed in a systematic way in school. In interviews, boys reported that when they were 'stuck' in their writing, they were encouraged to consult a friend on their table, the teacher, a dictionary or a thesaurus – but not to draw on their reading experience.

It is important to note that National Curriculum attainment levels in writing for both boys and girls lag behind their reading levels. This may imply that it is more difficult to attain the expected Level 4 in Writing at the end of primary school than to attain a Level 4 in Reading. Careful comparison of the criteria does reveal significant differences between what children have to do in order to attain a Level 4 in Writing, and what they have to do to attain the same Level in Reading:

Level 4 Reading

In responding to a range of texts, pupils show understanding of significant ideas, themes, events and characters, beginning to use inference and deduction. They refer to the text when explaining their views. They locate and use ideas and information.

Level 4 Writing

Pupils' writing in a range of forms is lively and thoughtful. Ideas are often sustained and developed in interesting ways and organised appropriately for the purpose of the reader. Vocabulary choices are often adventurous and words are used for effect. Pupils are beginning to use grammatically complex sentences, extending meaning. Spelling, including that of polysyllabic words that conform to regular patterns, is generally accurate. Full stops, capital letters and question marks are used correctly, and pupils are beginning to use punctuation within the sentence. Handwriting style is fluent, joined and legible.

In the reading assessment framework, children are expected not only to find their way around a text and retrieve information, but to call on their own resources and experiences and to use inference and deduction in explicating a text; their ideas and viewpoints matter. However, recent research has demonstrated that children may not need to deploy all of these skills in order to attain a Level 4 in reading. Mary Hilton's (2001) analysis found that the reading tests have become progressively easier for children. The number of questions requiring higher-order thinking skills – such as inference and deduction - have decreased each year since 1998, while the number of questions requiring lower-order thinking skills, where children are asked to retrieve information from the text, have increased. Hilton has called the reliability of the reading tests 'dubious', because in the 2000 reading test children could attain a Level 4 without demonstrating any powers of deduction or inference.

Even a cursory examination of the NC criteria shows that the requirements for Level 4 Writing are more extensive, detailed and complex than those for Level 4 Reading. In the writing assessment framework, children must simultaneously generate and control content, generic features, structure and transcription. Children's own views and experiences seem to count for less in this context. Both optional and statutory writing tests demand a great deal from developing writers, who must demonstrate all this knowledge and skill in a single piece of writing, against a checklist of criteria, in timed conditions, and without preparation.

The teaching of genres

The imbalance between reading and writing results may also be partly explained by the very rapid coverage of writing genres seen in the writing folders in most classrooms. More than one Year 5 class was taught the writing conventions of science fiction, Greek myths, journalism, advertisements, metaphors and instructions in the space of five months, as well practising for optional Qualifications and Curriculum Authority tests (QCA 2003).

Spring term first half	Spring term second half	Summer term first half	Summer term second half
science fiction; metaphors; Greek myths; poetry – Lulu, the Highwayman; story writing; dialogue; description	seal stories; advertisements; jingles; information; instructional writing	QCA practice and QCA test	Sachar novel; writing in role as refugee; writing as Victorian children; description of dance performance; letter to performer

Teaching a wider range of genres – especially non-narrative genres - is thought by many to favour the needs and interests of boys, but too fast a pace is almost certainly detrimental to underachievers. Weaker writers barely come to grips with one genre before they are faced with the next one.

A feature of the National Literacy Strategy is often to introduce and teach each new writing genre with a new text or text fragment. This may not always be a supportive way of working for underachievers. In project classes, where children wrote over a longer period in different voices and formats around the same text, children could draw together their ideas and use these to develop longer pieces of writing. A good example of this was Teacher P's 'Lulu' writing where the study of the poem generated notes in role, emails, extended descriptive writing and letters to the author. Writing around a familiar text enabled weaker writers to work within different genres without having to tackle new texts at the same time.

Teacher Assessment

Ongoing, formative assessments do not count in statutory assessment. Teachers (eg Teachers G and K) who keep formative assessments use them to write end-of-year reports, for parents' conferences, or to inform other school professionals such as LSAs, SENCOs or EMAG teachers. This has created a situation in which teachers actually *know* what boys are capable of in literacy but are unable to make this count in statutory assessment.

> Teacher S: "*I know they can do so much better. It's so difficult when my opinion is so different to the test score they get.*"

> Teacher L: "*They are so much more able than they are on the QCA papers.*"

> Teacher G: "*We know exactly what they can do, exactly where they're at.*"

It was interesting that Teacher S felt it was her 'opinion' that was different from the statutory assessment. She did not refer to her professional judgement or to the evidence on which it was based. Yet because teachers do know their pupils well, and have seen a range of their work in the context of their everyday learning, they often feel, with some justification, that they have a more complete picture of children's development than statutory tests provide. None of the project teachers felt that the QCA tests took proper account of what the focus boys had actually achieved over the course of the year. More holistic assessments, such as those provided by the CLPE Scale and the *Characteristics of Improving Writers and Writing Frameworks,* revealed that these boys *were* making progress in literacy, although not at the rate called for by the statutory assessment framework.

Differentiating 'underachievement'

If teachers did not intervene consistently in children's work, a large amount of work in the writing folders of focus group boys remained unfinished. The marking in these folders seemed to show that when boys wrote at length, this only created a string of errors which had to be corrected. If boys were starting from this point, it became increasingly difficult for them to take risks.

Many boys in the project wrote as little as possible, but each one for different reasons. Some, like Danny, wrote just enough to comply with the teacher's requirements in order to maintain peer group leadership and status. Others, like Okieriete, were discouraged by what they perceived as the long and drawn-out process of writing. Boys like Kenneth and Yusuf struggled with standard English spelling and sentence construction. Ashley and Ali were only just beginning to write legibly.

These difficulties were all, to varying degrees, factors in the boys' underachievement. However such different underlying reasons for low achievement were not detectable in their key stage literacy test scores, making 'boys' underachievement' appear undifferentiated and monolithic. Whenever teachers looked at children's texts individually, however, they could begin to respond to individual boys' needs.

Three boys: a range of improvement

Jermaine, Year 5: a plan that works and time to carry it out

Jermaine liked to write 'exciting stories' and had lots of ideas that he found difficult to control and sustain in writing. His drafts were often difficult to read and edit, and his writing would often stray far from his story plan.

He enjoyed illustrating his writing, as was shown in *Investigating Victorian Toys* in the Spring term where he drew much more than he wrote. The drawings have clear lines and a feeling of spaciousness and ease, unlike his writing.

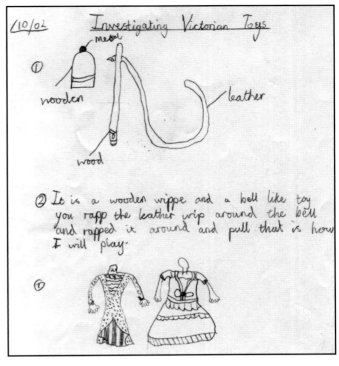

A mind-map proved to be the structure which helped Jermaine to organise his ideas effectively. This kind of structure seemed to work for Jermaine because it was a visual plan and had elements of drawing in it. Jermaine could see his ideas and refer to them in a non-linear way. Teacher S organised an extended teaching sequence around 'The Seal Wife' that included visualisation, whole class and group discussion, drawing and illustrating, using ICT, publishing, and reading to an audience. Jermaine benefited greatly from all of these experiences before, during and after his writing. He recognised the importance of visual planning for him and he now prefers to use mind mapping to plan for other types of writing in school.

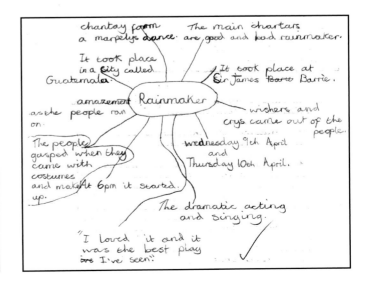

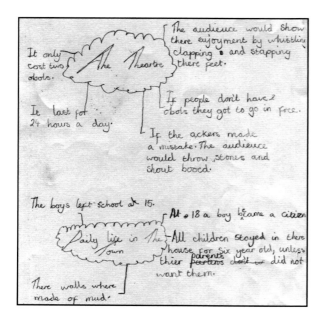

The story Jermaine wrote in response to 'The Seal Wife' (page 57) is a sophisticated narrative in three chapters. There are no echoes of the original text here – Jermaine has appropriated the story and made it completely his own. The first two paragraphs, in which no action takes place, create a lonely, desolate world. The tone becomes more optimistic in the third paragraph, when the fisherman wakes up and "... *he saw that the sea was unruffled and the sun was shining and the sea washed up green seaweed. The rock pools had little fishes and lobsters.*", but an ominous note returns as the fisherman steals the seal woman's coat and "*The waves started clashing, bashing and roaring as the fisherman ran home.*"

On the night after the children find her seal coat, "*this most glamorous thing*", the seal woman leaves her land family to return to the sea: "*The next morning they woke up to expect a nice breakfast but she wasn't there. The place was not clean or tidy. They ran up to their dad's bedroom. "Dad, dad, mum is gone!" cried the children.*" There is humour and suspense in the depiction of the fisherman awakening: "*What, what you must be joking" yawned dad. The dad got up and went down the stairs tripping up on the way. They searched and searched, trashing the place, the kitchen, bathroom and the bedroom.*" But the seal wife has not abandoned her land family completely. In the final paragraph, the fisherman stands alone on the shore, glimpses a seal slide into the water, and realises he is not alone.

Jermaine needs extensive preparation for this level of high-quality independent writing. He has not yet achieved the quasi-automatic control of transcription that independent writers need, and continues to make a substantial number of spelling errors. He exemplifies the great difficulty that many children have in controlling all the aspects of writing at the same time: content, organisation and transcription. Frank Smith's (1982) formulation, that transcription will suffer the more a writer focuses on content and vice-versa, would appear to describe Jermaine's situation. Jermaine also continues to be a 'slow' reader, finding it difficult to grasp the meaning of unfamiliar texts. Opportunities to reflect upon and discuss the seal story in depth were what helped him to develop his ideas for story-writing.

An improving writer

Jermaine is a self-motivated writer and one who shows all of the characteristics of an improving writer. He can write at length and has his own style. He chooses language for clarity, effect and meaning. He reflects on his writing and revises it for readers. He needs support with structuring complex stories, but this can be from his peers as well as his teacher. He shows increasing involvement and experience as a writer. However, there is now a wide gap between Jermaine's one-off high-stakes assessed literacy in test scores and the literacy of which he is truly capable. When asked about his QCA writing test, all he would say was that

> "*It was a bit hard because it was so quick, and it was timed as well. It was harder because it was timed. Usually you don't get it timed. I feel I did pretty good.*"

Jermaine needs time to think about his writing and develop it. Statutory tests deprive him of the possibility of preparing for his writing thoroughly – which he is learning to do, and which most adult writers do. However, his results on both his QCA tests and on the CLPE Writing Scale 2 showed he did make substantial progress in his writing over two terms. An analysis of his progress in relation to the *Characteristics of Improving Writers and Writing Frameworks* table reveal the areas where Jermaine is making most improvement.

Jermaine	January	July
NC Reading	2a	2a
NC Writing	2b	3b
CLPE Reading	2	3
CLPE Writing	2	4

> **Jermaine**
>
> - Characteristics: Increasing stamina, independence, involvement and experience as a writer
> - Texts longer, ideas more sustained
> - Language shows evidence of texts that have been read
> - Language uses written language forms and structures
> - Texts fully imagined
> - Evidence of attention to characterisation
> - Evidence of control of dialogue in narration
> - Texts show syntactic complexity
> - Texts cohesive between paragraphs
> - Texts show sense of reader and audience, language appropriate to genre and purpose
> - Texts marked for meaning with appropriate punctuation
> - Texts show range of spelling strategies and standard forms

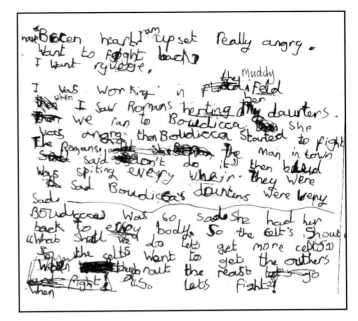

Ashley Year 4: developing stamina and control with support

As Teacher G noted earlier, Ashley's poor handwriting made it difficult to know what he could and couldn't spell and even to know what he had or hadn't written. His writing in March, "a design for an advert of 'Hombre' – a new product on the market", is a tangled mass of writing and drawing (see above and below).

Using the computer to word process motivated Ashley, although he still realised that good handwriting was an important skill to acquire. Opportunities to draft in a larger format also helped him to 'see' his writing, correct errors and make additions. Writing collaboratively gave Ashley more thinking time, enabling him to incorporate more of his ideas and create a longer piece of writing. He and Ali started by developing the 'pleading' dialogue between the Seal Woman and the Fisherman;

Ashley and ALI

The seal woman would say "PLEASE GIVE ME MY SKIN"

No! I am going to make you marry me first and you have to agree first ok or I will burn it"

LOOK I'M FROM THE SEA. IF YOU LOVE ME YOU WILL LET ME GO. WHY WON'T YOU? I GUESS I WILL MARRY YOU.

I need you, I have left my family and friends for you. OK I won't burn it.

THANK YOU FOR NOT BURNING MY SKIN.

Now let's get married tomorrow. The next day they got married and had children.

Using role-play, the two boys built their writing as dialogue. This writing is speech written down. They expanded this working relationship into the much longer *Letter from the Seal Wife to her Children*, in which their language shifted from speech-like writing to written language forms. The letter included narration as well as the voice of the seal wife:

(Ashley) *When the seal woman wrote a letter it said*

(Ali) ONE YEAR OLDER THE SEAL WOMAN WROTE A LETTER AND IT SAID

you will be growing fins children. You will need to go to the sea.

OR YOU WILL BE WOBBLING ON THE FLOOR *and so they went and jumped into the sea. But they could not find their mother so they came out and cut their fins off.*

THEN IT SAID "YOU SHOULD NOT CUT YOUR FINS OFF OR YOU WOULD NOT BE ABLE TO FIND ME" *So make another one. So they did it, and they said yes.*

And then they read more of the letter and it said I WANT YOU TO GO TO THE SEA AND PUT YOUR HAND IN / *in the waves and you will find seal skins. Give one to your father and your brothers and sisters so your dad knows I love him /* SO HE KNOWS I'M THINKING OF HIM BUT I AM STILL ANGRY AT HIM FOR TAKING MY SEAL SKIN

But the seal skin that I have for you will be in a mermaid shaped box WITH SIVER FINS AND GOLD FACE AND BODY. SO KEEP THE BOX.

There will be a box for each one of you WITH YOUR SKINS *and it will have names* IT WILL BE IN THE RIGHT ORDER, BIG TO SMALL TO MEDIUM. *the boxes are suitcases. when*

you put your skin come and visit me any time / ANYTIME YOU WANT IN THE ATLANTIC OCEAN.

PS I love you / AND GIVE THIS LETTER TO YOUR DAD TO READ TELL HIM I LOVE HIM TOO.

> The Seal woman wrote a letter and it said.....
> "when you are older, you will grow fins children. You will need to go to the sea or you will be wobbling on the floor"
>
> They jumped into the sea but they could not find their mother so they came out and cut their fins off.
> Then they read...
> "You should not cut your fins off or you would not be able to find me, so make another one"
> So they did it and thet said "yes" and then they read more of the letter and it said...
> "I want you to go to the sea and put your hand in the waves and you will find seal skins. Give one to your brothers and sisters, so your dad knows I love him. So he knows I am thinking of him but I am still angry at him for taking my seal skin. But the seal skin I have for you will be in a mermaid shaped box with silver fins and a gold face and body. So keep the box. There will be a box for each one of you with your skins and it will have names. It will be in the right order big to small and medium. The boxes are suitcases. When you put your skin on come and visit me any time you want in the Atlantic Ocean.
> PS I love you and give this letter to your dad to read. Tell him I love him too.

Ashley continued to benefit from writing with other children where he could contribute to and experience the creation of a whole text. Collaboration supported Ashley by giving him both space to think and an audience to reflect ideas. Writing conferences also helped him extend his independent writing, as two versions of the *Aboriginal Boy* text, written at the end of the Summer term, demonstrate. Ashley's first independent version was brief but to the point:

Aboriginal Boy
I am an aboriginal boy. I love sitting in the trees.
I like painting my body. I also love eating smoked
fish and love doing walkabout and doing
dreamtime. But I don't want a European to take my
country and tell me to put cloth on. I want freedom!

Good Day mate! I am an aboriginal boy called Natutu and I am ten years old. I love swinging in the long and powerful trees. I like painting my body with red, white, blue and green. I also love catching fish and cooking them on the fire. I love doing walk about and dream time.

Before a second attempt at this writing, an adult helper asked Ashley questions (eg "what kind of trees?", "what colours do you like painting your body?, What do you do in walkabout?") and he responded first verbally and then in writing. He asked the adult to scribe some sections, because he continues to find the physical act of writing extremely tiring. In this way he could see his writing take shape as he 'spoke' his text. This process also allowed Ashley to demonstrate more of his background knowledge of Australian speech forms:

Aboriginal boy
Good day mate! I am aboriginal boy called Natutu and I am ten years old. I love swinging in the long and powerful trees. I like painting my body with red, white, blue and green. I also love catching fish and cooking them on the fire. I love doing walk about and dream time. When I do walk about, my ancestors are discussing with me what they were and where they used to go. When I do dream time, I think of my ancestors and what they would have done before I was born. But I don't want a European to take over my country and tell me to put clothes on. I want freedom! We can accept you in our country but we don't want you to take it over and tell us what is not natural!

Ashley's Aboriginal Boy text gained in purpose and meaning by being part of a larger canvas of class writing linked to a picture book *Where the Forest Meets the Sea* (Baker 1987) about the destruction over generations of a rainforest. Each child in the class wrote in role as one of the characters or creatures in this picture book – a bird, a dinosaur, a tree, a tourist, a child, etc. Ashley's fragment is coherent in itself, and it is a significant improvement on where he was as a writer only a few months earlier, but - like the voices in 'Seal Wife in Divorce Court' - Ashley's fragment takes on more coherence and power in the context of other writing read aloud, like that of his partner Ali who wrote as 'The Forest':

The Forest
I could hear a chainsaw and a lorry in the distance, people saying "Bring it forward, now back, go this way, now back." Once I'm gone I'm gone. There's no way back. I would rather have a beautiful forest and beach than a stupid 6-star hotel. You cannot climb trees, you have to walk up and down stairs. Where will the aboriginal people go, where will the animals go?

Becoming independent

During the two terms of the project, Ashley becomes increasingly willing to take risks with composition and transcription. As well as simple narratives he is trying out new forms of writing, drawing on models in the classroom and on peer support. He still finds it difficult to sustain initial efforts over longer pieces of writing, and his sentence structures are still close to speech. However, he demonstrates increasing stamina for writing. His writing makes more sense and is becoming more coherent as he writes more. He shows greater awareness of spelling strategies. Ashley continues to enjoy a range of picture books for reading. He needs substantial support to sustain independent writing at length. Despite all these indicators of growth and development, after much focused preparation in the test format, he slipped back in National Curriculum attainment following the optional Year 4 QCA writing test. This did not reflect his substantial progress in writing over two terms as seen in his class work and in his assessment on the CLPE writing scales.

Ashley	January	July
NC Reading	3c	3a
NC Writing	2b	2c
CLPE Reading	2	3
CLPE Writing	1	2

> **Ashley**
> - Characteristics: Increasing confidence and stamina as a writer
> - Texts become longer, ideas more sustained
> - Texts more coherent and make sense
> - Texts more fully imagined
> - Texts show range of spelling strategies and standard forms

Yusuf Year 5: becoming engaged

At the beginning of the project Yusuf was a disengaged writer who wrote very little. All of his writing from December to April, when word-processed, fits onto two pages of A4. He writes a fragment of a story, two short pieces about 'The Future', a newspaper story about the Lady of Shalott, and fragments of writing about history and science topics. He never really seems to get going.

Yusuf's writing, December to April:

December 2002
Blodin the Beast the final Day
[Teacher prompt]
[Hosea stared at the water "But I cannot swim," he cried.]

Shanga wasn't dead, he was live. "You can swim," said Shanga in a louw vose. He put the carpet down and the carpet turned in to a spear. It wasn't a ourdernare spear. It was a magic spear. Hosea through the spear at Blodin and Blodin die. Hosea jump in the water and swim. *To Be Continued*

January 2003
The Future
One morning in the Year 2150 I got woke up by my brother Mohammad.
He shouted, "Wake up, Wake up breakfast is ready Mum at work."
"Okay" I said as I yawned.
Then I walked sleeply down the stair.
Then after I brush my theath I ran to my table. "Hay get the hovr reay" I shouted. Yes sir it said. Last one three is a rotte egg. Then when we went to school with my hover skaktbrode. Mohammed was a rootte eeg. I ran to my class. Then When I went to the class the teaching said to me "go to the History kabrode". I can to the History kabrode to get Herry VII Book. In the middle of the room was time warpe. I jumped in to it and I was in the Year 2003. Then I went to my havfe skateboard and everybody was looking at my and take about me. *To Be Continued*

The Kings
On the plant Earth there was a boy called Younis. He had short hair, big eyes, long legs, red jumper and bac troses. He buy a spaceship and the next day I want to space. And I ceck the ship and I went mewik I look at the last room and there was a time machine and I did no what it was. I push a button and I went way way way in the future on another plant I was scread. And I ran out of fas and I carsh and I was not dead but the ship was broken and I said to me slef how am I going to get home and the Galactic Lord come. Everyone bawd down but I didn't. They got out there gun and I telproted and I end at a house. I onep the door and eveone were having a war and some people die and some didn't and I was the King Ganymede Git and The Galactic Lord has the King of other world. They wer enmes. The End.
(teacher's written target: I will check through my work to make sure it makes sense to the reader)

February 2003
Mysterious Lady Breaks free
The Lady of Shalott was seen when the sun was riseing. The Lady Shalott was last seen flouting down the streame as pale as a Ghost I think she hasn't eat for a very long time.

March 2003
Leisure and Entertainment
On Saturday afternoon people like going to sporting events and horse rase football macts. The fist football cuble were at church chapel school.

March 2003
Life Cycle of a flour
Seed dispersal
The seed fully grown in to a sunflower by falling on to the ground. When the seed go on the ground it get coute in ananen frer and whe it get on the ground it the to germinating.
Germinating
Germinating mease when it start grow the thing it need to grow it need minerals water and sunshine it is called Germinating.

April 2003
Dear children,
    Befor you were me and your fater meat in the beach and I was dasing in the sea with me friend and we were

In May, Yusuf wrote at more length, working in collaboration with Lizzie. Together they created a 'seal wife' story on the computer. This text is longer and sustains a more coherent narrative than any of Yusuf's previous writing.

The Seal Woman (by *Lizzie* and <u>Yusuf</u>).

It was a sunny morning and <u>an old</u> <u>fisherman decided to go for a walk</u> <u>on the beach.</u> *He was looking around when he saw a group of* <u>normal</u> *people dancing.* <u>He looked very surprised and</u> *speedily* <u>walked over to them.</u>

<u>When they saw him they dived towards a</u> <u>pile of seal skins.</u> *One of them did not take their skin; they stopped and looked at the fisherman.* <u>The fisher-</u><u>man grabbed her skin</u> *immediately.* <u>The</u> <u>sea woman begged, "Please, please my</u> <u>skin give it to me."</u> *The fisherman did not care a bit.* <u>He pulled the sea</u> <u>woman by the wrist and took the lady</u> <u>to his house.</u> *As the years went by they got married and had children.* <u>The children were not sea people but</u> <u>they had a little web between their</u> <u>fingers.</u>

One day the fisherman decided to go shopping. While he was at the shops the children decided to play hide and seek. As soon as the game began they ran in to the barrels and found the seal skin. They ran to the kitchen and showed it to their mum. <u>Their</u> <u>mum was shocked</u> *and so relieved. She took the skin and hugged and kissed them. She waved goodbye and ran to the beach and as she ran she said to her children. "Every night* <u>at ten</u> <u>o'clock</u> *come to the beach and you will see me."* <u>The children did not</u> <u>understand their mum, but did not get</u> <u>a chance to ask questions.</u>

She ran to the beach <u>and pulled on</u> <u>her skin.</u> *Suddenly* <u>she spotted the</u> <u>fisherman in the corner of her eye</u> *and called out to him* <u>"I love you</u> <u>but I have always loved my seal</u> <u>husband more."</u>

Their story, like other collaborative writing in the project, showed signs of growing control and sophistication in comparison with the writers' previous work: it included mental state verbs (*shocked and relieved*) that tell readers more about the character, and literary language (*Suddenly she spotted the fisherman in the corner of her eye and called out to him*). Yusuf responded to his writing partner: they modified language, changing *a fisherman* to *an old fisherman* and introducing other words and phrases (*normal, speedily, at ten-o-clock*) to bring more detail to the text. Their story included two brief breaks in the time sequence (*The children were not sea people...The children did not understand their mum...*) that slow the narrative pace and provide more background for the reader. In the last line the writers recalled the original text (*I love you but I have always loved my seal husband more*). Yusuf and Lizzie also began to write sentences that start with suspense-building clauses: '*As soon as the game began...*', '*While he was at the shops....*' The influence of story-telling was evident throughout in the language and structure of the writing. However, it was impossible at this point to tell whether the improvements evident in this writing would be continued in Younis' independent writing.

But in June, quite suddenly, Yusuf began to write daily, independently and with enthusiasm in response to the Louis Sachar novel. He especially enjoyed writing and drawing in Bradley's "diary", which was not in his Literacy folder (where writing was marked and targets were set). His spelling improved as he wrote daily in familiar language about a novel that engrossed him.

Bradley's Diary

Speech bubbles on drawings of Bradley's toy animals:

You're the best in the wild wild west!

Not him again!

Wot the baby again!

You're the clever boy

Wow he's the best

He's crying again

I bet he's ripped up his language test

Great food Bradley

Maybe if you weren't so rude to your dad you wouldn't be crying

Bradley don't cry like that

Maybe you should not lie so much Bradley

Bradley you know your mum told you that she would take you to the zoo, you know she's a liar

Maybe lying is not such a good idea

Bradley you're good at lying, maybe you can think of something

5 June
My Embarrassing Moment

(writing prompted by Bradley going into the girls' bathroom in the novel)

One Saturday night I was at the cimars and I was a bit late. I was sototo be at the cimars at eight o'clock. When I saw down someone farted behind me and everyone was looking at me. They laughed at me and when it was finished my friend did fart noises and everyone went outside laughing and I was so embarrassed.

10 June 2003
Bradley visits the counsellor

[Teacher prompt]

[The door of the office was open, so he walked right in]

and saw a red headed, freckled faced lady on top of a ladder, fixing boxes. She turned around and said to Bradley, "I didn't hear you come in as I was hard at work."

"So! You asked me to come, so here I am" said Bradley in a mocking tone.

"Let me get one thing straight, when you're in my office speaking to me, you speak with respect just like I will speak to you." replied Carla in a calm voice. Surprised and shocked, Bradley said, "OK". "Right, let's get started". Bradley went and sat on the opposite side of the table from Carla. "Now what type of boy are you?". "A bad boy and I'm in a dumb office!". "Well have you got any friends?" "No, who needs them?"

12 June
Dear Diary

When I first went in there I thought she was a counsellor with a bad temper that shouted a lot. She told me to sit down and then I asked her am I going to break your cup, and then I thought she would blow her top but she didn't, and she said that I could break anything I wanted. After she said 'do you want to draw a picture', she wanted to have it and I said NO and the bell rang.

16 June
Jeff's thoughts

When I first went in there and looked at Miss Ebble, she had a rude expression on her face and I knew she was a rude teacher. When I came in she didn't say hello. She put me in the middle of the class and she said "Have you been to the White House?" and I said "no" and she said "There is no place you can sit, so you can sit next to Bradley" " Nobody would like to sit next to him, he's a bully" some one said. Then I sat down and I felt really sorry for him and I said, "I don't really mind". He replied by saying "SO". And when the school bell rang I walked to him. "Do you want to be my friend?" I asked. He said "Give me a dollar or I will spit on you". I gave him a dollar and ran. Now here is the really embarrassing moment. I was going to the counsellor's office and I ran down the corridor and I slipped and bumped my head and I still have the bump.

20 June
Dear Diary

After school I was going to Jeff's house to do homework, and I was going to beat up the girls. When I went to them, they kicked me and pushed me in the water.

20 June
Bradley returns home
[Teacher prompt]
[Bradley got his keys and opened the door]

eagerly and ran up stairs crying and shut his door with a "bang", and his mum came up stairs saying, "You're crying". "Am not" he shouted, "go away", and his dad came up stairs and opened the door and said "why are you crying?" "I thought I closed the door - because I beat up some girl and I got beat up by these big brothers and that's why". Then mum said "Why are you crying?". "Because the girl kicked me, it was four vs one and they pushed me in the water. " "My poor baby, I will go down stairs to get you some hot chocolate. I promise not to tell dad." I will get them back, he said to himself.

16 July
Dear Diary,

Today I feel like a new boy that is a little bite sad. Because Jeff has got new friends and he forgot about me and he is even starting to be rude to me and starting to lie like I used to. Loser! And I think in my way I am starting to improve. I think Carla likes me and I am starting to like her. Today Jeff had a black eye and he told his friends and they want to beat me up. I went in the girls bathroom and nobody was there. The girls came. I ran into the toilet and I came out and I thought they came out and they screamed loud.

Yusuf wrote *as* Bradley in his 'diary', and wrote reflectively *about* Bradley in other writing. His enthusiasm for the novel triggered his enthusiasm for writing. Writing daily developed his stamina; his spelling also improved as he wrote nearly every day in accessible language. Yusuf, like several of the focus boys, struggled with standard English spelling and sentence construction. An effective way for him to address these issues was though daily writing practice. O'Sullivan and Thomas' study of children learning to spell looked at the role of reading in developing spelling, and also highlighted the importance of writing regularly and at some length for children as spellers. (O'Sullivan & Thomas 2000: 94). If children do not write often and freely, taking risks with spelling, their understandings of spelling do not become apparent, they cannot be helped to correct their errors, and they lack practice in spelling.

Yusuf's enthusiasm for writing was also generated and sustained by Teacher K's consistent use of drama (hot-seating, thought-tracking, discussions in role) after reading - and before writing. This work in drama brought the Sachar novel alive, and Yusuf was transfixed by it. For the first time, he said, he was reading a book about 'a real boy' like himself. No literacy experience can be more relevant.

When we examine the full range of his writing over two terms, we can see that Yusuf is widening his range of writing and beginning to consider appropriateness of language and style. He is learning to link and develop ideas coherently. He is drawing on his experiences of reading in his writing. He is learning to revise his writing. His writing shows growing evidence of attention to characterisation and dialogue. As he writes continuously and at more length, his spelling improves; by the end of the year it is mainly correct and continuing to improve.

As a writer, Yusuf is becoming more engaged and self-motivated. His stamina is increasing and he can concentrate on writing for longer periods. Unlike many of the focus boys in the project, Yusuf did not practise for QCA tests in the Summer term, and yet he made gains both on the National Curriculum levels and on CLPE scales.

Yusuf	January	July
NC Reading	2a	3a
NC Writing	2c	3b
CLPE Reading	2	3
CLPE Writing	2	3

Yusuf

- Characteristics: Increasing confidence, stamina, independence and involvement as a writer
- Texts become longer, ideas more sustained
- Language shows evidence of texts that have been read
- Texts more coherent and make sense
- Texts more fully imagined
- Evidence of attention to characterisation
- Texts show growing sense of reader and audience, language appropriate to genre and purpose
- Texts show range of spelling strategies and standard forms

How can we see real children in numerical assessment?

These three case studies reveal the actuality behind apparently similar test scores and the differences between underachieving learners - their different strengths and needs. They reveal the different paths that learners take, and the experiences that can *make* a difference to their learning.

But they also highlight the fact that different forms of assessment tell us different things.

The writing which arose from project interventions was the result of many opportunities to talk, to visualise, to act out, to plan and draft in an open ended way, and to write over days and weeks in different modes and formats. It was therefore interesting, and concerning, to compare this writing with that done in the QCA writing tests which boys subsequently took in the summer term. The discrepancy between these two kinds of writing, done in such different conditions, must reflect the time it actually takes to become a writer. Teachers under pressure to get children to 'perform' to a high standard of writing in test conditions were depressed by the contrast between the writing test and what children were able to achieve in more favourable conditions.

There was no clear pattern in the progress recorded on National Curriculum Levels for the case study group (page 24). Most boys' results went up, but some went down, and others made no change. This contrasted with their results on the CLPE Writing Scale 2, and with the features of improvement that we discerned both in their writing and their writing behaviour. It made both the teachers and the research team question whether these kinds of NC tests are appropriate or reliable assessments for developing readers and writers, especially those with literacy difficulties.

Writing during the two-term project from these boys, who have very low assessed levels of literacy, show what is possible in (Barrs 1990) *normal tasks in favourable contexts.* The difference between these collections of writing and their QCA test papers is the difference between writing which is the result of extensive experience, discussion, preparation and feedback – and writing which is done for high-stakes assessment, with little or no discussion, preparation or feedback.

These observations may not be original, but in the current context of primary school assessment, they are perhaps worth making explicit. As a consequence of the introduction of the 'optional' QCA tests, most children are now preparing for SATs-like statutory tests in every year of the primary school – far more frequently than originally envisaged in the framework for national assessment. If their writing were improving as a consequence of this annual testing, the tests might be justifiable. Our evidence was that, rather than helping them to make progress, the tests were both failing to reflect their real progress, and were also taking up substantial amounts of class time.

Although project teachers recognised the value of creative approaches to literacy, they were in many instances hamstrung by the statutory assessment model. Most teachers felt pressured to teach to the QCA tests, even though they were theoretically 'optional'. Five out of six classes did intensive preparation for the QCA tests; *four out of the six classes sat mock tests as well as the real tests.* Because of this intensive practice, weeks of teaching and learning time were lost.

There are huge differences in how far individual teachers are able to exercise professional judgment in marking the optional QCA papers. Very different marking practices were adopted in the four different schools. Assessment has rightly been characterised as 'the secret garden' of education. In this garden, apparently objective scores may conceal substantial differences in the ways in which assessors interpret the marking criteria.

Teachers may be left to themselves to mark the papers, or may have to conform to a series of checks and balances. Moderation may reveal major differences between teachers' standards of marking. Where teachers' interpretations of marking criteria differ from those of others, they may come under pressure to 'standardise' their marking, so as to avoid discrepancies. And when children's marks are the basis of future targets, a tension can be created between teachers' desire to record children's achievement, and their knowledge that high marks may result in impossibly high targets for the following year.

The amount of teacher time and thought that went into arriving at reliable test scores in the project schools was substantial, and yet the tests themselves provided teachers with no new information about children's abilities. Far more could be learned about their progress from looking at their collections of writing and at the aspects of their improvement revealed by the CLPE Writing Scale 2 and the *Characteristics of Improving Writers and Writing Frameworks* (page 86).

Overall, the focus group of 24 boys did improve in literacy, but in small increments compared with their peers. They are not where the statutory assessment framework says they should be, and the gender gap remains. School literacy for many of these boys is a lengthy developmental process. Their long-term progress will depend not just on working with one teacher over two terms, but on teachers working together across age phases and year groups. It is however important to see that their writing is improving, and that these improvements can only be reliably seen in a collection of work over time. The breakthroughs that some achieved in the course of the project – Jermaine's successful adoption of visual planning formats, the improvements evident in Ashley's collaborative writing, the dramatic progress made by Yusuf writing as a direct result of his reading of the Sachar novel – were hopeful signs of what they were able to achieve in 'favourable contexts'.

9

CONCLUSIONS AND REFLECTIONS

ontinuity is a crucial factor in addressing the difficulties of underachievers. The importance of continuity was demonstrated particularly in the school where two teachers kept the same classes for an additional year after the end of the project and were able to build on their previous experiences. They explained to the research officer how this was working:

> Teacher G: "*I'm trying to be more relaxed about boys getting up and moving around; I think they need to do it – it's like having a brain break. I do a lot of collaborative work and writing in a bigger format really helps some boys see their work clearly for the first time, from there they can start to improve it. If you put the spade work in, you get results, but it takes time. And what I've learned with writing is to always make it high status, like when I say 'We're going to perform this!' "*

> Teacher P: "*While the project gave me a focus on the achievement of boys, the implementation of it really benefited the whole class – they all enjoyed it…The fact that I was focussing on a particular group of boys led me to give them roles in class that I hadn't done before. It made me realise that I should have stretched them more previously. For example, Benny – he didn't try hard and didn't seem to be bothered. Once he began to see success in some of the project work, he began to want more. He didn't have quite the problems that Bradley (the character in the novel) had, but there were some similarities.*"

In other schools, boys went into their new year groups with new teachers who did not continue the intervention approaches. The new teachers reported that these classes were "very skilled in discussion" and had "lots of ideas and things to say", "they really know how to talk about a story", "they can imagine what a character might say", (Year 6 teachers, schools C and D). But these observations were overshadowed by the drive to prepare these Year 6 children for Key Stage tests: "my job is to get them ready for SATS (statutory tests) in the spring".

Teachers who had taken part in the project adopted the intervention approaches that had been used with their new cohorts of children. They had discovered a way of teaching that made sense to them and that seemed to support children's progress:

> Teacher L: "*Word and Sentence work flow from the talking about the story or whatever they're reading and with their questions – it's building on what they know and it's linked to what they're reading and talking about. You can start teaching things that come out of the text. You're actually teaching them what they need to know at that moment and they can put it into their writing straightaway. I'm never going back to how I used to teach.. Before this, I was the teacher I never wanted to be.*"

> Teacher K: [as literacy co-ordinator]
> "*I'm developing a new scheme of work for English now for the whole school. The targets [of the NLS] were inappropriate for them [EAL and asylum seeker pupils], it doesn't help them, it's not where they're at, at all. The word and sentence goals aren't right for them. They need so much more experience reading and talking before they write.*"

Returning to the research questions

This project hypothesised that reading and writing as social activities were not being fully explored and exploited in the literacy curriculum, and that boys in particular were underachieving in this context. Interventions made by the project targeted boys, within the context of whole class teaching, to see whether increased opportunities for talk and interaction could create a more inclusive literacy curriculum.

Over two terms, a wide range of data was collected from teachers and boys in six Key Stage 2 classrooms. Recorded talk between teachers and children and between children formed an important part of this data. These opportunities for talk led to many different outcomes in writing. Perhaps more importantly for case study boys, such opportunities also created openings for boys to participate more actively in school literacy learning.

With these outcomes and openings in mind, we looked again at the research questions.

How does oral rehearsal - reading aloud, a range of discussion opportunities, and forms of drama - encourage underachieving boys to respond to texts and prepare for writing?

Oral rehearsal highlights the social dimensions of literacy, dimensions which motivate children to become literate. We found that effective oral rehearsal gave underachievers time to formulate a response to what they were reading and opportunities to bring their own experiences into discussions of reading. Teachers were crucial models of how these discussions might take place and go forward. The 'Rules for Talk' formulated by the project classes also helped to keep discussions on track. When Teacher L organised single sex 'Talk Tables' for literacy, results were positive as boys began to listen to others, share, and compare responses. Whole class 'Book Talk' helped to engage classes with the study of texts and generated extensive discussion. Teachers found that these oral approaches to literacy led to a more sustained focus on whole texts and less of a focus on word and sentence level text features. Children who became engaged with texts through this kind of talk went on (like Benny of the 'trouble boys' page 48) to refine and develop their ideas in a range of writing.

Forms of drama, at their most basic level, allowed children to get up from their chairs in what was often a sedentary curriculum; it was physical and enjoyable. As B. said, *It actually makes you WANT to come to school.* Through role play and enactment underachievers more fully imagined and entered the world of the text and this often gave them (as with Rammone page 42) opportunities to get more involved with school literacy. Drama and role play led, sometimes spontaneously, to drama on paper, as with Omar's 'Lulu' writing (page 43). Teachers

also noted that opportunities to enact the text could generate bursts of writing as children planned their dramas. Drama brought out the 'voice' of the text; with the support of this kind of learning even boys with special literacy needs, like Ashley (page 44), could acquire the language of the text and take on the voice of its characters. Through collaborative drama and readings, underachievers were able to be a part of and contribute to a larger text, as in Teacher P's 'Seal Wife in Divorce Court' (page 60)

Oral rehearsal demands a focus on the language of the text and this encourages children to hear different forms of English and expand their language for writing. Boys like Okierete and Kenneth (page 82) began to pick up on literary language under the influence of a text which had been retold around the class.

In two terms, the more time underachievers spent in a pre-writing phase - developing ideas through discussion and drama, making notes and drawings, collecting ideas and images, collaborating to brainstorm or draft a fragment of a bigger narrative picture, reflecting with an editing partner, emailing questions and receiving a response – the greater was the positive impact on their writing. Jermaine's discussions with a partner, his mind-mapping and the illustrations with which he punctuated the final copy of his 'Seal Wife' story, all helped him to develop his ideas fully and create a complete and sophisticated narrative (page 57). Literacy teaching that incorporated these kinds of experiences before, during and after writing allowed time for ideas and skills to take root and grow. Extended 'teaching sequences' from some of the classes involved in the project demonstrate how teachers were able to build on and extend children's literacy work through the use of discussion, visualisation, ICT, drama and role play, and publication (page 34).

How does creating a visible audience (through performance) or a virtual audience (using ICT) for reading and writing affect boys' perceptions of literacy and their achievement?

Boys were motivated to create high-quality texts when they knew these would be published or performed. Performance requires both an audience that listens, sees and responds and performers who read, enact, or speak in role. All parties to a performance therefore contribute something, and the process gave writing a clearer context and purpose for many boys. In performance, underachievers took responsibility for their ideas and their texts; it was an active experience in which children literally heard their own voices in their performed writing. All children enjoyed opportunities to present their work to an audience in this way. Teacher G's class insisted on videotaping their performed stories and spontaneously brought props to school to enhance the performances. Publishing also provided children with the opportunity to present their work to others. The children in Teacher S's class combined these two forms of presentation when they gave public readings of books they had written and designed (page 56). Using ICT for communication built on boys' engagement and expertise with this form of literacy and the extent of their home use of ICT as established by our interviews. It encouraged their ownership of writing both at the macro (whole text) and micro (spelling, punctuation) levels. Learners like Ashley and Ali (page 47) were helped by writing collaboratively on the computer, and by engaging the spell check and grammar check functions of the computer program. Interactive uses of ICT (email, screen and web reading, web publishing) offered weak readers and writers opportunities to 'play' at literacy whilst simultaneously engaging in 'real' literacy. Boys who shunned literacy were drawn into writing emails (page 72) and displayed unaccustomed interest and perseverance in this form of literacy. Email, in fact, became a key route to improved literacy achievement for many of these underachievers, as when the children in Teacher S's class began enthusiastically to write emails to Bradley Chalker in Louis Sachar's novel (page 72). This kind of literacy avoided the 'too easy, babyish' label which can de-motivate so many underachievers. Web publishing was also a hugely motivating factor in encouraging boys to write. With the project website, children knew that anyone anywhere – including parents - could see and read their literacy work.

How does collaboration and peer support help boys' literacy development?

Peer support can take many forms: it can be social or have more purposeful reading, editing or writing outcomes. Boys welcomed a brief time away from teacher-initiated reading and teacher-driven assessment, as a marker of their trustworthiness and maturity.

Teacher P's 'trouble boys' reading group enjoyed their status as a self-monitoring group and wrote up their reading notes regularly (page 65).

The most effective forms of collaboration underpin literacy development by integrating speaking, listening, reading and writing. Collaboration marks the fact that literacy is an active, social practice and the primary classroom is a site of constant and complex linguistic activity and interaction, even when children are not 'producing' anything in writing. Collaboration can take many forms (discussing, editing, brainstorming, group reading and writing, performing) and can take place at any stage of the reading or writing process.

In the *Promoting Boys' Literacy Learning at Key Stage 2* project, teachers observed that the negotiating skills required for effective collaboration had a positive impact on boys' behaviour as readers and as writers. When they organised 'talk tables' (Teachers S,K and L) or collaborative drafting or writing (Teachers G and P), children working together were seen to achieve more than they were able to do by themselves. Collaboration extended the writing process and made the decisions involved in writing more explicit for the writers. Collaboration created spaces where writers could continue a narrative thread, and contribute or alter ideas, phrases and vocabulary. Weaker writers, like Ashley and Yusuf, were obviously helped by writing with a partner. The syntactic complexity of their texts increased, and their narratives became more coherent. Inexperienced writers were also supported by taking part in the creation of a whole text and experiencing the 'big picture' of the text, as in Teacher G's Rainforest writing (page 93).

What is appropriate assessment?

Underachieving boys in this project were shown to be making progress, but at a slower pace than that called for by the statutory assessment framework. Their improvements could only be reliably seen in a collection of their work over time, and by looking at their long-term behaviour as readers and writers. Teacher assessment often seemed to be at odds with the results of statutory assessment in this area. It appeared that the current summative testing framework may not be appropriate, or reliable, for readers and writers with literacy difficulties. This project has offered evidence to show that a model of literacy based on teaching discrete skills to match measurable targets, which is assessed by one-off, high-stakes tests, may not be engaging children sufficiently with literacy learning. It may be especially ineffective in engaging the hard-to-reach boys who were the subject of our study. During the project we worked with a model of literacy based on boys' interests, needs and on inter-active approaches to learning. We used frameworks for assessment that reflected primary school children's progress and registered what they were actually capable of, in normal tasks carried out in favourable contexts.

Speaking and Listening has been the Cinderella of the English curriculum. Primary school performance tables show attainment for English (DfES 2003a), and individual schools and LEAs may show separate attainment scores for Reading and for Writing, but the third statutory section of the National Curriculum for English is virtually never shown – perhaps because it is teacher assessed (there are, as yet, no standardized, timed tests to measure speaking and listening) and successive governments have viewed teacher assessment as unreliable. In light of the latest QCA materials on Speaking, Listening and Drama (2003b), there needs to be a robust discussion about how something as ephemeral as *talk* may be reliably assessed, what kinds of evidence would be appropriate, and where and how these would be integrated with current assessment for reading and writing. In the 21st century it should be possible to consider videotape, audiotape and CD-ROM as ways to record and assess a range of speaking and listening - yet these formats do not enter into current statutory assessment procedures.

Boys: can and do

This project demonstrates that underachieving boys, with time and preparation, 'can and do' engage with reading and writing in school. They can and do imaginatively enter the world of a text, they 'can and do' enjoy a range of narrative fiction, they 'can and do' write with increasing independence, confidence and control. In order to create these conditions, project teachers moved away from the Literacy Strategy timetable, while retaining broad Literacy Strategy objectives. They included boys in whole class teaching that made time for children to talk, think, discuss, enact and interact around reading and writing. Project teachers did less 'transmission' teaching and created more opportunities to listen to and observe children in literacy work.

Not all project interventions were successful in all project classrooms, and teachers often felt more comfortable with some approaches and texts than others. However, in all cases, effective teaching was far removed from the 'bite-size chunks' and 'memorizing abstract facts' approach sometimes advocated in discussions of raising boys' achievement. The interventions made connections between children's social practices (talk, home and community experiences, play and movement) and school literacy practices, between children's social texts (websites, games, media, email) and school literacy texts.

Interaction of the major factors; the big shapes of an inclusive pedagogy for boys

In classrooms where targeted boys improved within whole class improvement, all children had opportunities to

- Develop ideas and language for writing through extensive, open-ended discussions
- Enact texts through forms of drama and role play
- Write at length over days and weeks in a range of collaborative and independent formats
- Write in different voices around the same text and bring these together for a whole class purpose or performance
- Collaborate for support and for enjoyment
- Regularly access ICT for discussion, independent and collaborative writing, and ownership of the writing and editing process
- Perform and publish their texts
- 'Play' at writing

These activities were promoted through

- Planning which was open-ended and flexible
- Focusing on the process as well as the product of literacy development, particularly writing
- Teachers engaging with children's resources and experiences

This research and intervention project offers evidence of the value of paying attention to the interactive aspects of becoming literate, and of the time it takes for teachers to develop these practices fully and effectively: literacy as meaningful discussion, drama, performance, ICT to communicate, reading and writing collaboratively for support and enjoyment. The different teaching sequences (page 34) show that teachers can use these approaches imaginatively and flexibly, adapting them to the needs and abilities of their classes. Through oral and interactive approaches, literacy can be seen as a social as well as a cognitive process, and above all, a long-term developmental process for children who may be underachieving and, as a result, may become disaffected.

Although questions about which types of text might inspire boys were not on the research agenda, it was apparent that boys became involved in school literacy when literature was introduced. The three texts in the project were very different: a mystery poem, a traditional tale and a contemporary novel. Yet they had this in common: they were high-quality, whole texts that teachers used to teach literacy to the whole class. Whole class teaching with high quality literature offers a different approach to tackling underachievement: rather than giving boys text fragments ('bite-size chunks') and narrow targets in order to assure their success parameters, teachers in this project included underachievers in a wide range of imaginative and purposeful reading, writing, speaking and listening experiences.

Although this was a small-scale project, working mainly through case study, the data from these urban, multiethnic classrooms do provide an authentic picture of children and teachers learning more about literacy. In looking at boys less as behaviour problems and more as challenges to the offered literacy curriculum, schools may reflect on the extent to which changes to this curriculum could positively impact boys' underachievement. Teachers may also use these snapshots of classroom reality to reflect on how far school literacy is engaging underachievers, and on what active interventions and changes to teaching are necessary to move those children who are on the margins into the centre of literacy learning.

BIBLIOGRAPHY

Allan, M. (2003) *Pick Up A Pencil* Hamilton: South Lanarkshire Council Education Resources

Alloway, N., Davies, B., Gilbert, P. & King, D. (1996) *Boys and Literacy:* Meeting the Challenge Canberra: Commonwealth of Australia

Anderson, M. (2003) 'Reading Violence in Boys' Writing' Language Arts January 2003 80(3)

Applebee, A. (2000) 'Alternative models of writing development' in Indrisano, R. & Squire, J. (eds) *Writing: Research / Theory / Practice* Newark DE: International Reading Association

Arendt, H. (1958, 2nd edition 1998) *The Human Condition* Chicago: University of Chicago Press

Arnold, R. (1997) *Raising levels of achievement in boys* Slough: NFER

Babbage, J. (1999) *Using Email To Assist Reading* A research project funded by the Teacher Training Agency as part of the Teacher Research Grant Scheme 1998/1999. London: TTA

Baker, J. (1987) *Where the Forest Meets the Sea* London: Walker Books

Barrs, M. (1990) *Words Not Numbers* Sheffield: NATE

Barrs, M. (2000) 'Gendered Literacy?' Language Arts March 2000 77(4) pp287-293

Barrs, M. & Cork, V (2001) *The Reader in the Writer* London: CLPE

Barrs, M. & Pidgeon, S. (eds) (1993) *Reading the Difference* London: CLPE

Barrs, M. & Pidgeon, S. (eds) (1998) *Boys and Reading* London: CLPE

Barrs, M. & Pidgeon, S. (eds) (2002) *Boys & Writing* London: CLPE

Bearne, E. (2002) 'Multimodal narratives' in Barrs, M. & Pidgeon, S. (eds) *Boys and Writing* London: CLPE

Baxter, J. (2001) *Making Gender Work* Reading: National Centre for Language and Literacy

Britton, J. (1980) 'Shaping at the Point of Utterance' in Young, R. and Liu, Y. (eds) (1994) *Landmark Essays on Rhetorical Invention in Writing.* Vol. 8. Davis, California: Hermagoras Press

Cameron, D. (2003) 'Schooling spoken language beyond 'communication'?' in *New Perspectives on Spoken English in the Classroom* London: QCA

Causley, C. (1996) 'What has happened to Lulu?' in *Collected Poems for Children* London: Macmillan

CLPE (1996) 'Primary Language Reading Scales' in Barrs, M., Ellis, S., Kelly, C., O'Sullivan, O. & Stierer, B. *Using the Primary Language Record Reading Scales* London: CLPE

CLPE (1997) *Primary Language Record Writing Scales 1 & 2* London: CLPE

Chambers, A. (1993) *Tell Me: Children, Reading and Talk* Stroud: Thimble Press

Coates, J. and Cameron, D. (eds) (1988) *Women in Their Speech Communities: New Perspectives on Language and Sex* New York: Longman

Connolly, P. (1998) *Racism, Gender Identities and Young Children: Social Relations in a Multi-Ethnic, Inner-City Primary School.* London: Routledge

Crossley-Holland, K. (2001) 'Sea-Woman' in *The Magic Lands* London: Orion

Daly, C. (2002) *Literature search on improving boys' writing.* For Ofsted (2003) *Yes he can. Schools where boys write well* London: Ofsted

Dawes, L., Mercer, N. and Wegerif, R. (2000) *Thinking Together: A Programme of Activities for Developing Thinking Skills at KS2* Birmingham: Questions Publishing Thinking Together Website: http://anubis.open.ac.uk/thinking/index2.html

DfEE (1998) *The National Literacy Strategy* London: DfEE

DfEE/QCA (2000) *The National Curriculum for English* London: The Stationery Office

DfEE (2001) *Guidance on the Development of Early Writing in Reception Classes* London: DfEE

DfEE (2001) *Developing Early Writing* London: DfEE

DfES (2002) *The Code of Practice for Special Educational Needs* London: DfES

DfES (2003) *Excellence and Enjoyment, a strategy for primary schools* London: DfES

DfES (2003a) *National Key Stage 2 tests for English performance tables* London: DfES http://www.standards.dfes.gov.uk/performance/ap/

DfES (2003b) *Using the National Healthy School Standard to Raise Boys' Achievement* London: DfES
DfES Gender and Achievement website:
http://www.standards.dfes.gov.uk/genderandachievement/

Dyson, A.H. (1988) 'Appreciating the drawing and dictating of young children' Young Children 43(3)

Epstein,D., Kehily, M., Mac an Ghaill, M. and Redman, P. (2001) 'Boys and Girls Come Out to Play: Making Masculinities and Femininities in Primary Playgrounds'. *Men and Masculinities.* Special Issue: Disciplining and Punishing Masculinities. 4(2) pp158-72

Ficher, R. (2002) 'Boys into writing: raising boys' achievement in writing' in Williams, M (ed) (2002) *Unlocking Writing* London: David Fulton

Galt, V. (2000) 'Diversity in the classroom; characteristics of elementary students receiving special education: boys outrank girls in behaviour, language problems' Education Quarterly Review March 6(2)

Gillborn, D. and Gipps, C. (1996)
Recent Research on the Achievement of Ethnic Minority Pupils.
London: Ofsted

Gillborn, D. & Mirza, S. (2000)
Educational Inequality: Mapping Race, Class and Gender
London: Ofsted

Glaser, B. & Strauss, A. (1967) *The discovery of grounded theory; strategies for qualitative research* Chicago: Aldine

Goetze, S. (2002) 'Children's Literacy Perceptions as They Authored with Hypermedia' Meridian: a middle school computer technologies journal. An electronic journal a service of NC State University, Raleigh, North Carolina; forthcoming in print: Volume 5, Issue 1, Winter 2002
http://www.ncsu.edu/meridian/win2002/513/index.html

Goodwin, P. (1999) *The Articulate Classroom*
London: David Fulton

Gordon, E. (1997) 'Sex, Speech and Stereotypes: why women use prestige forms more than men' Language and Society 26 pp47-63

Graham, L. (1999) 'Changing practice through reflection, the Key Stage 2 Reading Project, Croydon' Reading 3(3)

Graham, L. (2003) 'Writing Journals: an investigation' Reading 37(1)

Grainger, T., Goouch, K., Lambirth, A. (2003) 'Playing the Game Called Writing: children's views and voices' English in Education 37(2) pp4-13

Graves, D. (1983) 'See the Writing Process Develop' in *Writing: Teachers and Children at Work*
Portsmouth, New Hampshire: Heinemann

Green, C. & Green, S. (2000) *Assessment of literacy in the text level strand of the national literacy framework at Key Stage Two: issues surrounding genre and gender* European conference on educational research. Edinburgh: Primary Assessment Unit

Hannan, G. (2003) in Wilce, H. (2003) 'Putting the class back in our boys' The Independent 27 November 2003

Harris, R. (1995) 'Disappearing Language: fragments and fractures between speech and writing' in Mace, J. (ed) *Literacy, Language and Community Publishing*
Clevedon: Multilingual Matters.

Heathcote, D. (1980) *Drama in Context*
NATE Papers in Education. Sheffield: NATE

Hester, H. (1990) The Stages of English in *Patterns of Learning: the Primary Language Record and the National Curriculum*
London: Centre for Literacy in Primary Education

Hewitt, R. (1990) 'Youth, race and language in contemporary Britain: Deconstructing ethnicity' in Chisholm I, Büchner P, Krüger H. H., Brown P. (eds) *Childhood, Youth and Social Change - A Comparative Perspective* London: Falmer Press.

Hilton, M. (2001) 'Are the Key Stage Two Reading Tests becoming easier each year?' Reading 35(1)

Holden, C. (1999) *'I'm not good at holding a pencil': the underachievement of Year 4 and 5 boys in English*
Exeter: Project JUDE, School of Education, Exeter University

Holden, J (2004) *Creative Reading. Young people, reading and public libraries* London, Demos

Holland, P. (2003) *We Don't Play With Guns Here: war, weapons and superhero play in the early years*
Milton Keynes: Open University Press

Ishani, L. (2003) Keynote address to the CLPE Head Teachers' conference *Raising Achievement of Black Caribbean Pupils* November 14th 2003 (unpublished)

Kempe, A (1999) 'Drama in and out of the literacy hour' <u>Literacy Today</u> no 21. Available via www.literacytrust.org.uk

Lamprianou, I. & Boyle, B. (2003) *The effect of aspects of curriculum on the National Test results: the case of state primary schools in England* Manchester: Centre for Formative Assessment Studies, Faculty of Education, University of Manchester

Lincoln, Y & Guba, E. (1985) *Naturalistic inquiry* London: Sage Publications

Mac an Ghaill, M. (1994) *The Making of Men: Masculinity, Sexuality and Schooling* Milton Keynes: Open University Press

McGuinn, N. (2000). 'Electric communication and under-achieving boys: some issues' *English in Education,* 34(1) pp50-7

McKenley, J., Power, C., Ishani, L. and Demie, F. (2003) *Raising achievement of black caribbean pupils: good practice in Lambeth schools* London: Lambeth Research and Statistics Unit

Martin, N. (1987) *'On the Move'* in Goswami, D. & Stillman, P. (eds) (1987) *Reclaiming the classroom; teacher research as an agency for change* Portsmouth New Hampshire: Heinemann

McFarlane, A., Sparrowhawk, A., Heald, Y. (2002) *Report on the educational use of games* Cambridge: Teachers Evaluating Educational Multimedia (TEEM)

Merchant, G. (2003) 'Email me your thoughts: digital communication and narrative writing' <u>Reading literacy and language</u> 37(3) pp104-110

Millard, E (1997) *Differently Literate: boys, girls and the schooling of literacy* London, Falmer Press

Minns, H (1991) Language, Literacy and Gender London, Hodder & Stoughton

Moss, G. (1999) *The fact and fiction project* Southampton: University of Southampton School of Education

Moss, G. (1999a) *Texts in Context: mapping out the gender differentiation of the reading curriculum* <u>Curriculum Studies</u> 7(3)

Mullis, I VS, Martin, M O, Gonzalez, E J & Kennedy, A M (2003) *PIRLS 2001 International Report: IEA's Study of Reading Literacy Achievement in Primary Schools* Chestnut Hill, MA, Boston College http://timss.bc.edu/pirls2001i/PIRLS2001_Pub_IR.html

Myhill, D. (1999) 'Boy Zones and Girl Power; gender perceptions and preferences in English' <u>Curriculum</u> 10(2) pp86-99

Myhill, D. (1999a) 'Bottom Set Boys' in <u>The Use of English</u> 50(3) pp228-240

Myhill, D. (1999b) 'Bad Boys and Good Girls? Patterns of Interaction and Response in Whole Class Teaching' <u>The British Educational Research Journal</u> 28(3)

Noble, C. and Bradford, W. (2000) *Getting It Right For Boys...and Girls* London: Routledge

Ofsted (1993) *Boys & English* London: Ofsted

Ofsted (1996) *The Gender Divide – performance differences between boys and girls at school* London: HMSO

Ofsted (2002) *The Curriculum in Successful Primary Schools* London: Ofsted

Ofsted (2003) *Yes he can. Schools where boys write well* London: Ofsted

Ofsted (2003a) *Expecting the Unexpected: developing creativity in primary and secondary schools* London: Ofsted

O'Sullivan, O. & Thomas, A. (2000) *Understanding Spelling* London: CLPE

QCA (2000) *Standards at Key Stage 2: English, mathematics and science* London: QCA

QCA (2003) *Year Five Writing Test and Assessment Framework* London: QCA

QCA (2003a) *Creativity: find it, promote it* London: QCA

QCA (2003b) *Speaking, Listening, Learning: working with children at Key Stages 1 and 2* London: QCA

QCA (2003c) *New Perspectives on Spoken English in the Classroom discussion papers* London: QCA

Reay, D. (1991) 'Intersection of gender, race and class in the primary school' <u>British Journal of Sociology of Education</u> 12 pp163-182

Rundell, S (2001) Able boys' literacy practices home and school. Suffolk Local Education Authority (synopsis in <u>Literacy Today</u> no. 28 September 2001)

Sachar, L. (2001) *There's a Boy in the Girls' Bathroom* London: Bloomsbury

Sainsbury, M. (2003) *Children's Attitudes to Reading*
Slough: NFER

Scieszka, J. Guys Read   http://www.guysread.com

Sewell, T. (1997) *Black Masculinities and Schooling: How
Black Boys Survive Modern Schooling.*
Stoke on Trent: Trentham Books.

Smith, F. (1982) *Writing and the Writer*
Heinemann 1982, London

Smith, M.W. & Wilhelm, J.D. (2002) *Reading Don't Fix
No Chevys: Literacy in the lives of young men*
Portsmouth, New Hampshire: Heinemann.

Somekh, B & Mavers, D. (2003) *ImpaCT2, Strand 2: Pupils'
and teachers' perceptions of ICT in the home, school and community* Coventry: Becta for the DfES
http://www.becta.org.uk/impact2

Steele, S. (2004) Keynote address to the CLPE conference
Writing and the Imagination 'Looking For Trouble: creativity
and writing' February 6th 2004 (unpublished)

Street, B. V. (2003). 'What's 'new' in New Literacy Studies?
Critical approaches to literacy in theory and practice'
Current Issues in Comparative Education, 5(2)

UK Audit Commission (2002) *Special Educational Needs:
A Mainstream Issue* London: Audit Commission

Vauxhall Talk Workshop (1974) In Our Own Voices.
London: ILEA

Warren, S. and Gillborn, D. (2003)
Race Equality in Birmingham, A Final Report
London: University of London, Institute of Education,
Education Policy Research Unit

Wells, A. (2003) 'Skills chief bemoans the 'daily grunt' '
The Guardian Education section 28 January 2003

White, J. (1996) 'Research on English and the teaching of
girls' in Murphy, P. & Gipps, C. (eds) (1996)
*Equity in the classroom; towards effective pedagogy for girls and
boys* London: Falmer

Williams, A. (1989) 'Dialect in school written work' in
Cheshire, J., Edwards, V., Münstermann, H. & Weltens, B.
(eds) *Dialect and Education: Some European Perspectives*
Clevedon: Multilingual Matters

Williams, A. (2001) *Talk Written Down? The influence of local
non-standard dialect on children's school writing* Paper to the
International Literacy Conference, University of Cape Town,
South Africa, 13-17 November 2001

Wood, E. (2001) 'The Roots of Underachievement of Boys
in Literacy in the Early Years'
Primary English Magazine 6(3) pp23-26

Wood, J. (2000) *A Marriage Waiting to Happen: computers
and process writing* Newton Massachusetts: Education
Development Centre. http://main.edc.org/

Younger, M. & Warrington, M. (2003)
Raising boys' achievement, an interim report for the DfES.
London: DfES